APPOINTED ROUNDS

Appointed Rounds, Michael McFee's beautiful, funny, and heartbreaking new book of essays is part memoir, part cultural criticism, and part song of praise for books themselves as physical as well as literary objects. The same perceptual transformative cherishing of the everyday and close-at-hand that one finds everywhere in all his poems is very much at the center of this lively examination of a writer's life. Whether he's guiding us through the working class world of his childhood in the mountains of North Carolina, or describing and finding poetry in the too-familiar and thus unnoticed physical properties of books themselves, in the much-loved but seldom looked-at materials that comprise his poetic and pedagogical day to day experience, McFee enables us to shake free of habitual perception and see as for the first time the most familiar things with an abiding sense of wonder. The gratitude that pervades sharpens his attention to the world we can't help but feel in relation to the book itself. Which is to say, it is a book to fall in love with, not merely read.

—Alan Shapiro, Kenan Professor of English,
The University of North Carolina at Chapel Hill

MERCER UNIVERSITY PRESS

Endowed by

TOM WATSON BROWN
and
THE WATSON-BROWN FOUNDATION, INC.

APPOINTED ROUNDS

Essays

Michael McFee

MERCER UNIVERSITY PRESS
Macon, Georgia

MUP/ P553

© 2018 by Mercer University Press
Published by Mercer University Press
1501 Mercer University Drive
Macon, Georgia 31207
All rights reserved

9 8 7 6 5 4 3 2 1

Books published by Mercer University Press are printed on acid-
free paper that meets the requirements of the American National
Standard for Information Sciences—Permanence of Paper for
Printed Library Materials.

ISBN   978-0-88146-638-6
Cataloging-in-Publication Data is available from the Library of
Congress

for Mickey Farmer Pruett,

most faithful correspondent through the years

CONTENTS

4.

5.

6.

ACKNOWLEDGMENTS

Some of these essays were originally published in the following places—many thanks to their editors and readers:

"Anthologizing" and "The Mail": *Epoch* (the first republished as a *Poetry Daily* weekly prose feature)
"The Blackboard" (as "Ode to the Blackboard") and "Gradebook" (as "My Gradebook and Me"): "The Chronicle Review" Observer, *Chronicle of Higher Education*
"For Doris": *North Carolina Literary Review Online*
"Just As I Am Not" and "My Inner Hillbilly": *Southern Cultures*
"The Smallest Talk: One-Line Poems": *The Writer's Chronicle*, Associated Writing Programs
"Proofs": *Carolina Quarterly*
"*Relief*": *Amazing Grace: North Carolina's Influence on the Writing Lives of 30 Contemporary Writers*, edited by Marianne Gingher (Chapel Hill: University of North Carolina Press, 2015)

Some of the poems in these essays have been published in the following places—thanks to their editors and readers as well:

"Saltine" (in "My Inner Hillbilly"): *That Was Oasis* (Carnegie Mellon University Press, 2012)
"The Death of Randall Jarrell" and "Frosted Windows in a Small-Town Presbyterian Church" (in "For Doris"): *We Were Once Here* (Carnegie Mellon University Press, 2017)
"Pilgrimage" (in "The Mail"): *First Things*
"Snow Goat" (in "My *New Yorker*"): *Vanishing Acts* (Gnomon Press, 1989)

The lines in "The Mail" from "Please Write: Don't Phone"—by Robert Watson, from *The Pendulum: New and Selected Poems*

(Louisiana State University Press, 1995)—are reprinted by permission of LSU Press. The monostiches in "The Smallest Talk: One-Line Poems" are reprinted as follows: "The Cathedral Is," from *As We Know* by John Ashbery. Copyright © 1979 by John Ashbery. Reprinted by permission of Georges Borchardt, Inc., on behalf of the author. "Silence," "Physics," "'To Thine Own Self Be True,'" and "Her Name," from *An Oar in the Old Water* by William Matthews. Copyright © 1971, 1972, 1973, 1976 by William Matthews. Reprinted by permission of Sebastian Matthews. "Elegy," by W. S. Merwin, collected in *The Second Four Books of Poems*. Copyright © 1960, 1961, 1962, 1963, 1964, 1965, 1966, 1967, 1968, 1969, 1970, 1971, 1972, 1973, 1993 by W. S. Merwin, used by permission of the Wylie Agency LLC. "A Deer," from *The Selected Poems of Yvor Winters* by Yvor Winters. Copyright © 1999 by Janet Lewis Winters. This material is used by permission of Ohio University Press, www.ohioswallow.com.

Finally, thanks to Alan Shapiro for his generous advice and comments. Particular thanks to Michael Chitwood, my first and best audience, who has—for decades—read everything I've written and helped make it better.

PREFACE

Though I enjoy public readings, I do worry about a writer over-introducing his work. Why explain what your written piece will soon demonstrate? Why tell what you're about to show?

I feel the same way about published books. I love sitting down to read them, in silence, alone, and I don't want the author announcing what this novel is going to do or whispering how to appreciate this book of poems before I actually get to a word of the text. If the book is well made, shouldn't its structure and meaning be clear to an attentive reader?

It may be a bit different with a collection of non-fiction. Sometimes, a few words up front can help orient readers before they set out into a book's landscape, can give them the big topographical picture before their feet hit the trail. There are many different terms for such preliminary (i.e., "before the threshold") material, each with its own shade of meaning and placement: *foreword* (usually by someone other than the author), *preface* (by the author), *introduction* (often a more extended part of the text itself), the nicely casual *author's note*. And there are other less bibliocentric approaches to preparing the way for the word: the dramatic *prologue* (literally, "to speak before"), the legal *preamble* ("to walk in front," like a tour guide), the musical *prelude* ("to play beforehand") or *overture* ("to open," from the same root as *aperture*).

If I were to write a preface for this book, it might go something like:

My title comes from the unofficial motto of the U.S. Postal Service: "Neither snow nor rain nor heat nor gloom of night stays these couriers from the swift completion of their appointed rounds." That's a stirring declaration, one I discuss later in section 23 of "The

Mail," and I've always liked its concluding phrase. All of us have "appointed rounds" in our lives, essential things we are given to do and must try to complete, whatever the inner or outer weather, whenever the time of day or night, however we may approach those duties. This is particularly true for writers, couriers who must fulfill their appointed rounds in words, working out their obsessions on the page, moving toward completion at a not-so-swift pace.

This collection of fifty essays—many of them pointed, a page or less, in the playful manner of Robert Francis and *The Satirical Rogue on Poetry*, and others rolling on for much longer—addresses the subjects I keep circling back to, stuff I can't stop thinking or caring about: books, my native mountains and state, writing, reading, teaching, and, yes, the daily mail. If *Appointed Rounds* has an elegiac air, I don't mean it to be of the cranky or rueful "I wish everything could return to the way it was" kind; these prose explorations, like my poems, are meant as appreciations, paying close attention to things that have mattered to me, savoring their details while exploring their larger design, and saving my versions of them even as they may change or fade or disappear altogether.

1.

A BODY

A book has a body, to which my body responds. It has, like me, an anatomy. Its spine in my hand is a familiar, sometimes intimate, fit.

Reading a book is a sensory experience. I take in its words with my hungry eyes; I hear the pages whisper as they turn; I touch it gently, beginning to end; I smell the tang of a new volume, the musk of an old one. And though I may not taste a book, I have been known to lift one to my lips upon finishing and kiss it, like a grateful priest after the Gospel reading.

A book's body, like mine, ages. Light hurts it, over the long haul: some hardbacks wear a jacket for protection. The pages of a book can yellow and crack and fox, developing stains and spots like the skin of the hands holding it. And yet the acid-free paper of the volumes I have written will survive me, which is a gratifying version of immortality, my name vertical on many spines instead of merely horizontal on a single gravestone. Even if no one takes those books down and reads them, they will exist when I do not.

Books are three-dimensional creations. That's how we 3-D creatures need to encounter them: in a world of height and width and depth, not on the flatness of a screen.

A bookshelf is a dormitory. Go wake a body up.

COVERS

O f course you can judge a book by its cover. It's a major part of the decision-making process for prospective readers, which is why presses go to the trouble of designing a distinctive word-wrapper that will attract the eye and hand: a good cover is like a visual blurb, opening a window onto the book or capturing some essential aspect of the work at hand.

Writers naturally fret about their books' covers—or, if they're lucky, their books' dustjackets, a term that sounds much more dashing and upper class, like something you'd wear in a mansion's library rather than something you'd spread over a lumpy bed. Though some publishers may invite input on cover design, the finished product is rarely how the authors imagined or desired it.

I learned that with my first book. My wife did a beautiful watercolor of the Blue Ridge Mountains and I sent it to the press, thrilled by the prospect of having that image launch my career. A week or so later they returned it, saying, "This is nice, but we can't afford to print the cover in full color." They asked her to simplify the image, which she did; but that was still too complicated. Finally, she reduced it to a grease-pencil drawing of a mountain range, and that's how they printed it, in library binding, as if it were a textbook.

Decades removed from my initial disappointment, that cover seems fine to me. Could it have been better? Definitely. Could it have been worse? No doubt. Through the years, I've come to accept that a cover isn't really part of the book that a writer writes, not in any organic or necessary way: a different designer, or the same designer on a different day, would arrive at a totally different concept from exactly the same text. A cover is an ex post facto shell: once someone starts reading, it's face down, out of sight, displaced by the words themselves.

But that doesn't stop me from fussing over my covers, and exasperating my publisher with questions and suggestions before the book is published. I want my books to be dressed as well as possible, to make the strongest possible impression out there in the cold, cold world, and father always thinks he knows best.

BY'S

The best word in the front matter of a book may be *by*. That durable little preposition is the hinge between title and author: this book is by this person; through the agency of "A," "*B*" was made. Even when it's only implied—"by" does not necessarily appear on the cover or title page—we know it's there, an everlasting bond connecting writer and written. And it's always part of the legal literary byline, as in my most recent collection of poems: Copyright © 2017 by Michael McFee.

By is minimal and powerful, composed of the second and the penultimate letter of our alphabet: it's not quite alpha and omega, or "a to z," but "b + y" is mighty close, and similarly comprehensive.

It has several other bookish shades of meaning. One is "according to," as in the Gospel According to (i.e., by) Luke; and verily, each published work is a distinctive verbal world according to its author—it is his account of how things are, at least on the page. Another, and the most personal meaning for a writer, is: "next to; close to." Once your book exists, it becomes a creature in the world, with its own life: it is your metaphorical child, one that is close to you, one that can possibly bring disappointment but is mostly a source of joy, satisfaction, pride. It stands by you, day by day. It is by your side, to the end. You would gladly put your hand on it and take an oath, by God.

FRONTISPIECE

"**F**acing title page" is disappointing as a term. Its location is clear enough, but the page lacks a name and identity all its own: it's defined in terms of its much more important neighbor across the spread.

Why don't we bring back "frontispiece" for the verso opposite the recto title page? It's a grand word, and it would bring a certain stateliness to the front matter of a book, evoking the tradition of magnificent authorial portraits whose precious ink was veiled behind a protective sheet of tissue, issuing an expensive, crinkly whisper when turned.

It would also be appropriate for what often appears on that page now, a list of books also by the author. Why? Because those previous publications are, in essence, an ongoing self-portrait in words. The volume readers hold in their hands is the latest version of the writer, but those earlier incarnations—however flawed—underlie the current likeness.

"Frontispiece" was originally an architectural term, for the decorative facade of a building. That metaphor might work as well. Each book an author publishes is part of a larger structure, another piece of the oeuvre-in-progress construction project that the public can behold and respond to. The frontispiece page reminds them what has already been built by the writer, its chronology of titles providing some context as they move past that facade and into the new building itself, the fresh interior space of an unread book.

TITLE PAGE

The title page is so much more than that.

It begins with the book's title, at the top of the page—a crucial piece of information—but it doesn't stop there. Next is the author's name: without this person, there would be no title and no book. And at the bottom of the page, anchoring everything, is the name of the publisher, without whom the book would not exist as a 3-D object. Technically, then, this is the title/author/publisher page, though it's more efficient to let the one word stand for all three.

The book's spine is a condensed version of the title page, with—for a skinny volume of poetry—the words rotated ninety degrees to a vertical axis and following each other rather than stacked up and spread out: there's the author, there's the title, there's the publisher, arranged so that they can be clearly read on a shelf, without having to open the book. The spine is a single informative line when the book is laid flat on a table.

The front cover is, typically, the top two-thirds of a title page, with the names of book and author displayed in clever, eye-catching, and (one hopes) irresistible fashion.

The truest title page in the book is the half-title page, the first actual page encountered when the book is opened, i.e., p. *i*: the only thing on it is the book's title—no subtitle, no author, no publisher, nothing but what the volume in your hand is named. For some reason, this is also called the "bastard title page," though there's nothing illegitimate or nasty about it. The half-title is a clean, clear, helpful introduction.

My favorite title pages are those that include the publisher's city: that gives the book a home, a place of origin. This can get out of hand—my trusty 1973 *American Heritage Dictionary* was published by "Houghton Mifflin Company, Boston/New York/ Atlanta/Geneva, Illinois/Dallas/Palo Alto"—but usually it's limited to a town or two at most. I like having a location for the press, an address for its volumes. I'm proud to have several books published by "The University of North Carolina Press, Chapel Hill and London." It doesn't matter to me if their London office is a locker in Victoria Station—I can say I've been published in England's capital, as well as in Macon, Georgia; Pittsburgh, Pennsylvania; Durham, North Carolina; Knoxville, Tennessee; Clinton, New York; Rocky Mount, North Carolina; Frankfort, Kentucky; and Orlando, Florida.

It's hard enough to title an individual poem, much less a whole book. I'm glad that titles have their own page, and I'm glad that the title page reminds us who wrote the work we hold in our hands and where it came into the world. That's a firmly rooted, almost biblical way to begin a book.

TABLE OF CONTENTS

It's such a tasty metaphor, right up front, the book's contents laid out for the reader like a feast covering the table with dozens of different dishes prepared and grouped and presented with great care by the cook: take, eat.

COPY RIGHT

Why should anyone pay any attention to the copyright page? It's the flip side of the book's single most important page, the title page, which tells you what the book is named, who wrote it, and what press published it where. That's essential: without such orientation, where would readers be?

Then you turn the page, and there on the back is a welter of information, in a smaller font size: can't you simply skip that stuff, like titles in a movie, and move on to the dedication page and the table of contents and, then, the sweet text itself, the book you want to read?

Sure. But there are little pleasures to be had on the copyright page.

One is the copyright line itself, the wonderful word "Copyright" followed by its equally wonderful symbol ©, that circled "c" followed by the date of publication and the author's or press's name. As an author, I prize that line. It says to the world: *I made this, it's mine, and if you want to use it in any way, you must ask.* It's a planted flag: "all rights reserved."

I also like the Library of Congress Cataloging-in-Publication data, all that bibliographic info, numbers and letters and words that will guide my book to its proper shelf-spot in libraries I'll never see, where it may be read by people I'll never know. It's a comfort to have the ISBN there, too, suggesting that what I wrote might actually be ordered by bookstores and purchased by readers. But then, I'm a lapsed librarian and bookshop clerk, a biblioptimist.

And I really like that "10 9 8 7 6 5 4 3 2 1" line. Technically, it's the printer's key, indicating which printing of the book you're holding; but couldn't it also be a kind of backwards countdown to blast-off? *Ladies and gentlemen, the book is about to lift from the pad!*

Though pretty much everything on the copyright page could be skipped by readers—it must be there, legally, though it doesn't affect your experience of the book in any significant way—its very name reminds you that the person who wrote the words you're about to read did his absolute best, through protracted verbal labor, to get the copy right.

ACKNOWLEDGMENTS

Before we tuck into a book's feast, the author must pause to say grace, to give thanks for what we're about to enjoy. That's what the acknowledgments page is, a recognition of others who helped make this meal—this finished arrangement of word-sustenance—possible. It's not a pious rote bowing of the stilled head, eyes shut, but a series of thankful nods toward those whose support might not otherwise be known: magazines and editors, who published early versions of the work, and also arts councils and foundations and endowments, as well as family and friends and close readers, all those indispensible sous chefs who pitched in along the long way, without whom this book would not exist.

In some books, these acknowledgments are listed not on a separate page, but included below the copyright material; in others, they come after the main text. Wherever and however they're presented, the principle is the same: sheer unself-centered gratitude. Amen.

BACK MATTER

Some terms used for the back matter of a book—that shadow or echo cast by the text—have a strangely anatomical tone. An *appendix* hangs upon the book like a vestigial organ. An *index*, like a forefinger, points the way back to specific pages. Even the notes would be *footnotes* if they were printed where their citations appear, a step down from the sentence to the bottom of the page and a smaller font.

Books of poetry don't usually require that kind of supplemental material, or a bibliography or glossary, though some collections do include notes about references in the poems, something the author wants to make sure the readers know. I always tell my students that—despite the inescapable example of T. S. Eliot and "The Waste Land"—they should avoid the need for footnotes or any extra-textual stuff to explain the brilliant intricacies of what they've written.

I'm grateful that *colophon* has no etymological connection to *colon*, though it also comes at the end. Instead, it's "a summit or finishing touch," the cherry on top of the book's sundae, containing happy facts about its publication, that happiest of facts. Three of my poetry collections have concluded with colophons, telling how many were published and who manufactured the physical volumes. Two were "composed in Bembo with Eric Gill's Perpetua used for display": such graphic specificity pleases me, as do the words "printed on acid-free paper," which means that those books—and my poems, inked onto their leaves—will long outlive me. And that, for a writer, is the heart of the matter.

AUTHOR'S NOTE

There's often too much or too little in the author's note anchoring the back of a book.

We don't really need to know where the author was born or now lives: if that's important, it will come out in the work. We don't really need to know where she went to school, or teaches, or works, if she works at all on anything besides books. We don't really need to know that he has a family, or pets, or other extracurricular activities, in order to comprehend the words between the covers. We don't really need to know the previous publications, or prizes won, or other honors and distinctions, to decide that this author is worthy and that we should go ahead and start reading. But such biographical information has become a staple of literary publicity, a way of establishing credibility and engaging the potential reader, along with an author's photo and some pithy jacket copy. These conventions seem unlikely to change.

A poet can dream, though, right? Since each book published is, however obliquely, an autobiography, a conversion of the author's real and imaginary life into words, perhaps the truest note might be the simplest: "[Name] has written [number of] books, including the one you hold in your hands, on which she worked for many years. Thank you, very much, for reading it."

—No, that sounds unsatisfying, somewhat high-handed and smart-alecky. But an author's note that tries to be funny or offbeat is even worse. And to have no bio info at all feels standoffishly weird: the author is not good old Anonymous, and the book sure didn't write itself.

I guess I should look on the bright side. For now, my author's note is a work in progress, a draft writer's-life-in-a-paragraph, which can still be revised. Once my dates are enclosed in parentheses, it's set in stone.

AUTHORS' PHOTOS

They can be unfortunate, these self-conscious likenesses at the back of the book.

Sometimes fingers are pressed to temples, as if the writers are feigning thinking, or as if their heads are heavy props they must hold up.

Sometimes the background (office, city skyline, nature) is much more intriguing than the sensitive figure in the foreground.

Sometimes the pose and smile are so artificially strained that the effect is taxidermal.

Sometimes the photo was taken so many years ago that, looking at picture and bio note, you feel like you're reading an obituary in a newspaper.

Most writers probably don't like having their picture taken at all, at least not to accompany something they've written. It's a visual version of an author's statements about a finished book: the image of the writer, and the intent of the writing, should be evident in the work itself without having either extracted for publicity purposes.

But that's what these photos are about: how a writer or publisher wants the public to see the author. They're promotional material. They're ads. Whitman was obsessed with pictures of himself, and kept at it until he arrived at the Good Gray Poet likeness that he craved. Decades ago, New York houses would dispatch Thomas Victor to take canonical photographs of their authors: to have his name as a credit line beside your picture meant that you'd made it, you were officially a member of the literary dream team.

Authors' photos are like casting a movie based on a favorite book: the results can be quite disappointing, the screen image much less satisfying than the page. But now and then they're not bad, if the photos manage to catch something genuine about the authors behind the words, a hint of a rumor of a clue about their real selves. That's what all writers hope for, though usually seeing our posed and shot body is like hearing our voice on a recording: *Really? Ouch.* That's when it's time to get back to the desk and disappear into our work.

BLANKS

E very book has blanks built into it.

The first and last of those empty pages—in hardback editions—are the endpapers, a heavier stock of paper that connects the cover of the book to the first and last pages. Authors may dream of having an elegantly marbled end leaf as the entrance and exit to their volumes, or some other sort of clever decoration or design, like a map or a family tree, but typically it's plain, durable paper in a solid color, something to help hold the book together. Endpapers are, in effect, the first three and last three pages of the book, a calming prelude before readers get to any text and a postlude once they're done. And in paperbacks there are no endpapers, just the uninked other side of the front and back covers.

The next blanks come somewhere in the front matter, e.g., facing the table of contents, as if the book is gathering its breath before saying, "Okay. Here's what you're in for."

Should there be a Section One page, a blank page will often precede and follow that numbered leaf: it's surrounded by blankness front and back, significant breaks in the volume's pace. That empty verso sheet before the first page of actual text is a final meditative pause and clearing of the mind before the first notes of the book's score are heard and felt.

Depending on how the text fits onto the leaves, there may be one or more concluding blank pages after the last page of actual text, a place where the book's final words can resonate, a brightness where the black ink can fade to white. It reminds us that any volume is as much white space as words, as much silence as sound, as much inarticulate and essential breath as actual utterance.

Without those blanks, those empty windows or mirrors, those moments of fruitful nothingness, a book might feel like too much unbroken text. With them, a book is—like a life—an ongoing balancing act, a chiaroscuro interplay of light and dark.

2.

MY INNER HILLBILLY

Dr. Julius Hibbert: Yes, I remember Bart's birth well. You don't forget a thing like…SIAMESE TWINS!
Lisa Simpson: I believe they prefer to be called "conjoined twins."
Dr. Hibbert: And hillbillies prefer to be called "Sons of the Soil," but it ain't gonna happen!
—*The Simpsons*, season 8, "Treehouse of Horror"

∧∧∧∧∧

In an interview a few years ago, I described my long-haired, flan-nel-shirted, lonesome undergraduate self as a "hillbilly doofus."

Where did *that* come from? Not the second word, "doofus," which was and is accurate, but the first: of all the words in the world I could have picked, why "hillbilly"?

∧∧∧∧∧

I grew up in the Blue Ridge Mountains, the son of a Bill from the hills. I drove a local stretch of US 25, the Dixie Highway used by mountain families emigrating north to Detroit, to find work in the factories and live in the hillbilly ghettoes there.

And yet I never used the term "hillbilly" or gave it much thought. I never read "L'il Abner" or "Snuffy Smith" on the comics page, I never ate Kellogg's Frosted Sugar Stars (cereal mascot char-acter: Hillbilly Goat), and I never saw a single episode of *The Bever-ly Hillbillies* or *Hee Haw*, because the nearby ridges kept our cheap TV antenna from pulling in CBS shows.

But even on trips into savvy Asheville, the images were there—for example, on Tunnel Road, at the Mountaineer Inn Motor

Lodge. It wasn't the illiterate backwards N's and E's on the tall sign that signaled "hillbilly": it was the scraggly-bearded Mountaineer himself, looming over the motel and road. He wore patched overalls, a battered hat, and an ambiguous expression—threatening or welcoming, hard to tell. In one hand he cradled a corncob pipe; the other circled the barrel of an enormous shotgun resting on its butt near his big bare feet.

∧∧∧∧∧

Surely my father and mother knew plenty of unstereotypical mountaineers, growing up in western North Carolina before the Depression. Their immediate families may have lived in town, in Asheville and Waynesville, but they still had plenty of country kin. All too familiar with that hardscrabble world, like other good postwar Americans they didn't want to raise their kids that old way. They wanted a new and finer life for their daughter and son.

That must be why Dad spent years converting our little log house, built by a Floridian to be a summer vacation cabin, into a comfortable year-round residence for us. That must be why Mom loathed country music—originally called "hillbilly" music—and why our loud, trashy, NASCAR-loving neighbors infuriated her. That must be why my mother went to such lengths praising any local manifestation of culture or elegance. "I'd scrub floors in the Biltmore House," she'd say, "just to be in such a place."

∧∧∧∧∧

I love a juicy etymology, and you might think that "hillbilly" has one; but not really. *The American Heritage Dictionary*, first edition, on my writing desk for decades, says it comes from "*hill* + *billy*, pet form of William." Whatever that means. *The Dictionary of Smoky Mountain English* says "origin obscure, attested only since 1900"—which makes it, ironically, a modern term. *The Encyclopedia of Appalachia* says it was first used in a New York newspaper to describe someone who "lives in the hills, has no means to speak of, dresses as he can, talks as he pleases, drinks whiskey when he gets it, and fires off his revolver as the fancy takes him."

So the noun "hillbilly" may have been invented by a twentieth-century Yankee, broadcasting the seeds of idle, uncouth regional stereotypes in his original description. Did that doom the word from the very start?

∧∧∧∧∧

I knew a real hillbilly kid when I saw one. Boys and girls alike looked different, smelled different, and acted different from the rest of us: pale, grimy, silent, peripheral—if they did show up at school, they didn't pretend to like it.

I remember a tall third-grader named Pearl, with scraggly white-blonde hair, who wore brogans and a threadbare floral granny dress and a thin, tattered sweater always buttoned up. Who knows how many times she'd flunked already, looming above her new classmates like an uneroded peak? Her neutral gaze and expression never changed, not even the day the teacher caught her copying her neighbor's test answers, word for word, including the other girl's name.

∧∧∧∧∧

I was on the square dance team in high school, and loved it. At the time, I didn't think, "This is an expression of my mountain heritage, and much more authentic than any made-in-Asia hillbilliana art or craft." What I did think was: All the really cute girls are square dancers, and this is my best chance to touch and clutch and spin these beauties, in public!

We were pretty good, the T. C. Roberson team, and we traveled around the hills for exhibitions and competitions, including the

Mountain Dance and Folk Festival, hosted by the ancient of days himself, the legendary Bascom Lamar Lunsford, who'd founded the festival back in 1928 and spent his long life collecting Appalachian songs. But we "smooth-style" dancers were mere shuffling posers compared to the clog teams and solo buck dancers, whose pounding rhythmical footwork shook the stages so hard you could see the boards shake and the dust fly: though no less patterned than our genteel routines, their loud, powerful stompings and bouncings seemed much wilder, scarier, almost primitive. And while their legs were flailing, their upper bodies remained still and their faces were always impassive: whatever true hillbillyness is, I was watching and hearing and feeling it anytime they danced.

It was on those stages that I started paying attention to the music itself, the songs deftly picked and fiddled by local groups, some of whom were genuine old-time players: while the beat carried us through our routines, the exuberantly melancholic notes and tone soaked much deeper into my body. That's the sound that now means *home* to me, a music of nimble hands over strings: it's all edge and pitch and headlong, heartfelt bittersweetness, like I'm driving fast on a narrow mountainside road with no guardrail.

∧∧∧∧∧

Shortly after we turned forty, my wife signed us up for a ball-room dancing class in Durham, where we live—a delightfully romantic idea. I think we were the only straight couple, and I know we were the worst, thanks to me. She learned the steps and turns perfectly from the first lesson, but I couldn't ever get the hang of it, mostly because I couldn't stop thinking and moving like a square dancer: I wanted to swing my partner, promenade, four-leaf clover, birdie in the cage, dive for the oyster, dive for the clam, open up them pearly gates...

I never felt less like urbane Fred Astaire and more like a hill-billy rube.

∧∧∧∧

I never considered myself a "Southerner" until I got to Chapel
Hill, where there were courses in such things as Southern Literature
and the American South, where the level of regional self-
consciousness was very high, and where there were more Yankees in
one place than I'd ever encountered, not all of whom took kindly to
the peculiar region where they'd landed.

I'd never really considered myself a "mountaineer" either, until
I got to UNC and discovered books by Robert Morgan and Fred
Chappell and Jonathan Williams on the library shelves, natives of
Appalachia who wrote excellent poems about its landscape and peo-
ple and culture: they made me really see and hear the mountains,
which I hadn't considered as a subject.

Recently, I dusted off the *Yackety Yack* yearbook from 1976,
when I was a senior, and turned to the photograph of the staff of
the *Cellar Door* literary magazine. Sitting on the dappled grass are
the fiction and poetry hotshots, the clever writers and critics, the big
scholarship winners and the out-of-state prep-school kids; standing
behind them and to the side, nearly out of the picture, is me—like
the hillbilly kids at my elementary school, I was pale (genes don't
lie), grimy (wearing a denim shirt and my patched pair of Levis),
silent (mouth closed), and peripheral (at the outer limits of the
group). I look like what I was, a self-conscious mountain boy who
knew his place.

And yet I'm smiling, at home at the margin, where all writers
like to be.

∧∧∧∧

Are hillbillies just hicks (the other h-word) at a higher elevation?

There's no shortage of terms for "inhabitants of a rural or remote area who are characterized by an utter lack of sophistication or

cultivation"—bumpkins, clodhoppers, crackers, hinterlanders, peckerwoods, provincials, ridge runners, rubes, sons of the soil, stump jumpers, yokels, and many others. And once you start looking and listening, the word "hillbilly" seems to be everywhere: in commercials, in *The Simpsons*, in a recent *New York Times* crossword puzzle where 14-down was "Hillbillies' cousins"—eight letters, starts with an R...right, "REDNECKS." I'm sure there must be shades of meaning for these hayseed terms, but when lumped together they sound like variations on the same derogatory theme.

At a big gathering of Southern writers, I once saw a writer weep over the use of the term "white trash"—she found it hurtful enough to make her cry, several times, in public and on camera. And *Appalachian Journal*, at Appalachian State University in Boone, has a spirited and often angry feature leading off each issue, called "Signs of the Times," where they document popular-media examples of the "cultural denigration" of Appalachia, especially images of the "contemptible rural unwashed." Should I be more like them, upset and vigilant and pissed-off about the careless or deliberate use of the word "hillbilly"?

∧∧∧∧∧

Once, an alert New York copy editor asked if perhaps I meant to use the word "spigot" at the end of the line "Mom held the long knife under the spicket"—warming it up before slicing some very frozen ice cream. I stood my ground and said, No, *stet* please, because that's the word the characters in the poem would have used. To its credit, the magazine said, Fine, and the poem appeared in the fall 1996 issue of *Hudson Review* with the common Appalachian word for a faucet, the more colloquial "spicket"—a small triumph for regionalism, right?

Not for long. I just checked that poem, "Yule Log," in my book *Earthly* (2001), and discovered that Carnegie Mellon University Press, of Pittsburgh, Pennsylvania, changed the terminal word of line fourteen back to "spigot," without asking me and without me noticing it until now. It's no big deal, it's only a couple of letters, the press was following standard usage and correcting a questionable spelling; but the tone is all wrong. The word that will outlive me, in the finished volume, is more like one that George Vanderbilt and his fellow aristocrats might have uttered at Biltmore Estate in the late nineteenth century than one that my poor hillbilly kin would have said ten miles south and many hungry years later.

∧∧∧∧∧

At the bucolic hilltop Virginia Center for the Creative Arts, several Aprils ago, two new writer-friends from New York and California called me a "hillbilly metrosexual." I laughed at the metrosexual part—nothing could be less likely—and at the oxymoron, which sounds like something that today's hipster Asheville might put on a bumper sticker.

I held my tongue about "hillbilly." Though I'd have swiftly corrected any mispronunciation of "AppaLAYchia," I said nothing about that part of their wisecrack. I didn't want to be rude to these urbane visitors to the Southern mountains, my native region, or to explain the vexed history of that word. But did I also keep quiet because I know I'm not really a hillbilly, any more than I'm a metrosexual?

Or is it actually the opposite—that, despite my suburban upbringing in the mountains and my decades in Piedmont academia, I knew the word was true to what I really am, at some essential level? Am I finally coming to terms with my inner hillbilly?

∧∧∧∧∧

There's no single "Appalachian accent," any more than there's a uniform "Southern accent"—it all depends on where you're from and who you grew up with and what stuck in your mouth and ear and brain. But in my corner of the North Carolina mountains, most of us articulated consonants and vowels, syllables and words, phrases and sentences in a certain way: both stretched-out and pinched-down, our speech could lull like a branch over rocks, but it never lost its chill, its edge.

That accent is difficult to describe or metaphorize. I know it when I hear it, and I used to speak in it, back when I was growing up but also when I went home for a while or talked on the phone with my mom or dad, my speech lapsing into those hillbilly patterns that no doubt amused or appalled the Chapel Hill globetrotters who overheard me saying "ink pen," "greezy," "might could," "plum crazy," "wadn't," "yonder." It would have displeased my high-school literature teacher, too, an elegant woman who did her best to strain local impurities from our south Buncombe version of the Queen's English. But my mountain family is pretty much gone, and my native dialect is, too, though that tongue or tone can resurface to surprise me now and then. I wish that happened more often.

∧∧∧∧∧

Can an outsider use the h-word without being offensive, any more than a white person can use the n-word?

Probably not.

Can "a person from a rural mountainous area, especially of the southeastern United States," to quote my falling-apart *American Heritage*, use the word "hillbilly" without being ironic or disparaging or self-loathing?

Possibly not, given the century of demeaning images that have barnacled themselves to the hull of this polysyllable.

And yet, unlike the n-word—which sounds like what it is, a vicious, degrading epithet that I can't bring myself to write or say—"hillbilly" itself is a not-unattractive sound. It fills the mouth nicely. It's got dactylic charm, and it sports two alveolar rhymes concluded by the upbeat "e" sound. It's a playful sequence of phonemes, much easier to say when self-identifying than "I'm an Appalachian-American" and much more colorful than "I'm from the mountains." It's fun to speak, a sober joke: "My name is Michael, and I'm a hillbilly."

∧∧∧∧∧

Last week I found an envelope with some black and white snapshots from half a century ago, from several trips our family made to Cherokee, North Carolina, three slow hours to the west of our house in Arden. In one picture, my sister and I wave from an overdecorated teepee's open "door." In another, I pose by a gift shop's totem pole, trying to make my face fierce as the creatures stacked beside me. And in the last one, my sister sits on the knee of a squatting man, a photo so heartbreaking it's hard to look at—because in this picture she's still alive, a grinning little girl wearing her cat-eye glasses; because the gift shop behind them, named "Pow-Wow," is crowded with customers and junky souvenirs, including corny hillbilly postcards; but mostly because of the Cherokee man himself. He's dressed in the same kind of shirt, slacks, and shoes that any American male might have worn in August 1956, but he's also wearing a huge feathered headdress that must have been cruelly hot and heavy in the summer. No doubt he wore it because it's what the tourists expected, because he had to make a living and support his family, and because it's what "redskins" did back then: wear feathers, and say "how," and pose for pictures with the white tourists whose ancestors drove their ancestors down the Trail of Tears...

His big hands carefully hold my sister. The sun further darkens his beautiful skin. He looks straight into the camera, his closed mouth hinting at the beginning of a smile.

∧∧∧∧∧

Are mountaineers to "hillbillies" as Cherokees are to "injuns"?

No. Absolutely not. Native Americans have suffered in ways we can never imagine, and to a great degree because of us, the emigrant Scots-Irish who poured down the Great Wagon Road and eventually displaced them.

And yet—in terms of the nation's popular culture, its versions and distortions of a people, its appetite for caricature—our fates are similar, if not equal. We've played the part if it paid and we needed to, in order to survive.

∧∧∧∧

"Hillbilly" could be a fightin' word, if delivered in the right (that is, the wrong) way, or if combined with the right (that is, the wrong) word: "stupid hillbilly," "hillbilly idiot," or any of a wide range of profanities used before or after it. If the right (that is, the wrong) person sneered at me and said, "You hillbilly moron," I'd be tempted to toss my beer in his face and take a poke.

But as a lapsed quasi-hillbilly of advanced age who wears expensive bifocals, I wouldn't. I'd try to turn his insult into harmless self-deprecation, a few laughs, something to snuff out the punches before they start. Isn't that another way to survive?

∧∧∧∧

I've lived in the Triangle area of North Carolina for more than forty years, but I've yet to stop yearning for the mountains. Other immigrants from the hills, like fellow writer Michael Chitwood, say the same thing: the Piedmont is a wonderful place to live and work, but it simply doesn't feel like home, deep down.

Maybe somebody should make t-shirts for us Appalachians-in-Exile, with the motto: STILL A HILLBILLY. I'd mean the last word, "hillbilly," not as caricature but as a suggestion of character: independent, peculiar, spirited, inventive, and very proud of where and what and who I came from. I'd mean the first word, "still," not as a moonshine pun extending the internal rhyme, but as a testimony to the power of place: I wasn't trapped by the hills, I got out, I made a good life elsewhere, but part of me will always be of the steadfast mountains, if not in them.

∧∧∧∧∧

I know there's a clear distinction between the terms "mountaineer" and "hillbilly." The former is more accurate and positive; the latter is exaggerated, negative, an offensive, cartoonish image of a poor, dumb, lazy feller who only rouses himself from nappin' or tendin' the still to go huntin' with his hound or flirtin' with his gal or feudin' with his gol-dern neighbers.

But I'm a poet, and—despite the ludicrous stereotypes—I can't help liking the word itself and what it does. "Hillbilly" conjures up more of an image than "mountaineer," in the same way that the word "cabin" makes a clearer picture and sharper sound than the phrase "vernacular log architecture." And whether used as noun or adjective, it's geography-specific, always (in my opinion) a strength, its syllables like blue hills receding toward the horizon.

I'm looking for the virtues in "hillbilly," the positives in the negative. Can this word be redeemed, reclaimed, used? Is it disingenuous, here in the hyper-wired twenty-first century, to adopt it as one's own?

∧∧∧∧∧

Sometimes, after I make an especially dark pronouncement or gloomy prediction, I'll shrug and say, "Well, I'm just a hillbilly fatalist." I inherited that philosophical predisposition from my mother, who could find the coal-black lining in any silver cloud. She believed, and a lifetime of disappointing experience had proved, that fate was waiting for you at every turn, ready to crush your spirits and prospects flatter than a fritter: you might as well accept and submit to it.

But Mom was a paradox. Despite her bleak streak, falling like a shivery mountain shadow over anything we mortals might try to do, she was hardly a passive woman: clever, tenacious, ambitious for us kids if not for herself, she never gave up. Despite the chip on her shoulder typical of some Appalachian natives—a sense of inferiority to the more educated citizens of the outside world, a persistent insecurity—she never backed down: though the situation might seem hopeless, she refused to surrender. Her specialty was feisty letters to the editor about local injustices and indignities, as she perceived them, including the mid-1960s chlorination of the local water supply.

In a way, she was the quintessential hillbilly, ignored or condescended-to or put-upon all her life, yet willing and eager to take a stand and fight, however foolish or doomed her efforts seemed. To use a term she applied to other people she admired, folks whose complicated personalities could accommodate considerable tension and contradiction: my mother was "a real character."

∧∧∧∧∧

I don't think about my inner hillbilly all that much. Some things will stir it up, though, and remind me of that private identity: a beautiful picture of the Blue Ridge ranges, say, or a few notes of that high lonesome bluegrass sound, or the slightly acrid and loamy smell of a rhododendron thicket.

Or—lately—food. I've been thinking about, even craving, some of the food we ate when I was growing up, which has led me to write about such fare as sawmill gravy, salted watermelons, and the humble cracker, the basic white Premium saltine by Nabisco:

Saltine

How well its square
fit my palm, my mouth,
a toasty wafer slipped
onto the sick tongue
or into chicken soup,

each crisp saltine a tile
pierced with 13 holes
in balanced rows,
its edges perforated
like a postage stamp,

one of a shifting stack
sealed in wax paper
whose noisy opening
always signaled *snack*,
peanut butter or cheese

thick inside Premiums,
the closest we ever got
to serving *hors d'oeuvres*:
the redneck's hardtack,
the cracker's cracker.

I may not have used the word "hillbilly" at the end of that poem—it didn't sound as good as the others, and didn't deliver the punch line—but believe me, that's the group I had in mind.

I know I need to be careful about my diet, and not eat too much salt or sugar or bleached flour or additives. Having lived where I've lived and done what I've done for so long, I know how to enjoy a pricey cracker with fancy toppings: I have shopped at A Southern Season, "Chapel Hill's Landmark Gourmet Market," without embarrassing myself or my companions. But a saltine feeds a hidden part of me in a way that nothing else can or ever will. It connects me to my childhood, and to my family, and to my family's family: a saltine is one small thing keeping that connection alive. It's beyond comfort food: it's communion.

∧∧∧∧∧

I'm not sure why I used the word "hillbilly" in that interview. It was unpremeditated tomfoolery. Maybe I was unconsciously echoing the *Seinfeld* episode where Jerry calls Kramer a "hipster doofus," and substituted one h-word for another. Or maybe I was goofing around with words, as usual, and liked the way "hillbilly" sounded with "doofus."

And yet—without stopping to think or censor—"hillbilly" was the word that came to my mouth, to characterize myself as an outsider among the sophisticates at UNC, way back when. I wasn't the first mountaineer to feel that way: another who did was Thomas Wolfe, fellow native of Asheville and Buncombe. Though Tom thought of himself as a city boy—unlike the "mountain grills" that his father railed against, those lazy, swinish rustics outside town— he was regarded as a kind of wild hillbilly giant in Chapel Hill. Hundreds of miles from "the hills that shut in Altamont," as he calls them in the first sentence of *Look Homeward, Angel*, Wolfe discovered his Appalachian subject matter and self-identity while starting out as a writer in college, back in 1916. His description of the native population around Asheville, at the turn of the twentieth century, is an insightful appreciation of hillbillies: "The hill and country people in the surrounding districts," he writes, "were Scotch-Irish mountaineers, rugged, provincial, intelligent, and industrious." I love how he uses the word "provincial" in a positive way, as a strength and not a limitation. Tough, rooted in their place, quick-witted, hardworking—that's the true hillbilly at his best, and the one I aspire to be, wherever I am.

I admit: I don't look or behave any more like one of those rugged "Scotch-Irish mountaineers" than Thomas Wolfe himself did. And yet both of us Buncombe County boys harbored an inner hillbilly, something that (much to our surprise) endured and deepened through long years away from Appalachia. Even if neither of us displaced natives could ever go home again, home never quite left us, and we never stopped longing for the hills. We kept going back to the mountains the only way we could, finally: through words.

JUST AS I AM NOT

Music is in the very air at the Billy Graham Library. From the moment you leave the massive asphalt parking lot, hymns rise like a holy fog from the ground, through squat green speakers lining the sidewalks and crossing the grass, constantly piping "Great Is Thy Faithfulness" or "All Hail the Power of Jesus' Name." It's vaguely soothing and a bit spooky, as if you're standing above a choir in a cavern, or walking over lost souls stranded in subterranean purgatory on the outskirts of Charlotte, who lift up their heads and sing to us humans still on the surface of earth:

Let every kindred, every tribe, on this terrestrial ball, to Him all majesty ascribe, and crown Him Lord of all!

+

Today is October 23, 2007, my mother-in-law's eightieth birthday. This day trip from Durham to the Library and back is her big gift. My wife and I have driven her here, a two-and-a-half-hour trip on busy I-85; another gift is that my wife's youngest brother, an investment banker in the Queen City, "surprises" us on the entrance sidewalk, to his mother's delight.

My mother-in-law belongs to a conservative Southern Baptist church, in which she and her husband (who died several years ago) raised their three children, none of whom are Baptists anymore. Through the decades, she has donated regularly to Christian organizations like Billy Graham's, so this is a pilgrimage for her, a visit to a sacred place: the home of the world's most famous and successful evangelist.

+

The first of the two buildings we enter, just past a split-rail fence, is the Graham Family Homeplace. That may conjure up humble, dirt-floor log-cabin imagery, or—given that Billy's family ran a dairy—a simple farmstead; but in fact it's a solidly middle-class, two-story house, moved here from a solidly middle-class Charlotte neighborhood a few miles away. The windows have trim black shutters, there are comfortable porches, and the gutters are in excellent shape (as a homeowner, you notice such things). Though only a few rooms are open to the public, you can peer into others, and if you're like me you think: Man, I wish I'd grown up in a place as nice as this.

Wherever Billy's religious convictions came from, they didn't arise from privation. If the preacher-to-be wasn't privileged, he certainly wasn't suffering either. His earliest origins on the dairy farm were likely more modest—like many non-urban Americans ninety years ago, he must have bathed in a washtub with his siblings, and used an outhouse—but once his family moved to this red brick neo-Colonial, when he was nine years old, there was nothing rustic about where he lived during his adolescence. The Graham Homeplace is surprisingly bourgeois.

+

We exit the back door of the house, through a screened porch. The sky can't quite decide whether to rain or not, but the singers underfoot never hesitate, blessing our ankles:
Then sings my soul, my Savior God to Thee, how great Thou art!

+

The second building we enter—looming behind the Homeplace like a shadow of the family's past, the hard work on the farm that made the fine house possible—is harder to fix in a phrase. On the Billy Graham Evangelistic Association (BGEA) website, it's described as a "barn-like structure" and a "dairy barn-styled library." It's not an actual farm building moved here from the Graham Brothers Dairy, though it's supposed to suggest that pastoral past in its general shape and size and appearance: it does have a gambrel roof (more typical of the northern United States than the South) made of a material resembling tin, and it does have reddish wooden siding. It's a barn in the way that Duke Chapel is a Gothic cathedral: it's not, really, but looking at it makes you feel like it is, brings up the desired visual and emotional associations.

So let's call it "the Barn."

Every barn has a door, a way for animals and feed and equipment to come and go. This one does, too. But since the Barn was constructed by the BGEA (founded in Minneapolis in 1950, moved here to Graham's hometown in 2003), even the way you enter and leave a building can be part of the organization's ministry, so that the Library becomes "a living crusade that will touch and change the lives of visitors," as was proclaimed at the dedication ceremony in late May of this year.

The etymology of "crusade" is "crux." It's easy to guess what that's Latin for. And so we enter the Barn through the cross—literally: a forty-foot-high, tinted-dark-glass cross, stretching upwards from the floor, in what would be the rose window wall at Chartres. The cross is cut into or out of that barn wall, as one might carve such a shape into a pumpkin, a thick cruciform pattern almost as tall and wide as the building: it's smokily reflective, it's striking, and it must be a pain to keep clean. Our little pilgrim band has to walk through a door in the foot of the cross to get inside. The symbolism is unavoidable.

+

I'd describe the interior design of the Barn as "modified Cracker Barrel." An antique carriage hangs from the ceiling, the rough-cut beams have been branded with Bible verses, and the walls are covered with period photographs and antique license plates and lots of old-timey tools—scythes, saws, axes, plows. There's a vintage Graham Brothers Dairy truck, and wooden crates and buckets and hay bales. Bird calls erupt from tiny speakers overhead now and then, as if sparrows have flown into the barn and roosted out of sight.

(If this were a movie, which it sort of is, we'd now hear the bomb-shelter chorus make a joyful noise on the soundtrack: *I sing because I'm happy, I sing because I'm free, His eye is on the sparrow and I know He's watching me.*)

This entrance area is meant to inspire a homey and nostalgic mood, to evoke the rural, unrushed, non-modern America of our grandparents, to inspire us to "step back in time" before we "follow the footsteps of Billy Graham through a life he could never imagine." Mostly, it makes me crave some buttermilk biscuits with sawmill gravy; but the empty Graham Brothers Dairy Bar in the far corner features generic fare, burgers and fries and Cokes.

+

Music haunts the men's room, too, words and notes doing what they can to deodorize the place and lift it to a more spiritual plane. The bathroom's design extends the barn motif, with splintery planks and corrugated tin dividing the stalls where you do your business while "Blessed Assurance" surrounds you:

This is my story, this is my song, praising my Savior all the day long!

+

The first stop on the tour is Bessie, a big animatronic Holstein waiting in her stall in the front corner of the Barn to talk about Reverend Graham as a child. Bessie's head *mooves* left and right, her lower jaw *mooves* up and down to approximate speech. She describes young Billy Frank's cold hands on her udder. She tells us that he practiced preaching to tree stumps and sometimes while milking her. Near the end of her monologue, she praises "the pure milk of God's word," a somewhat opaque and unpasteurized metaphor.

Bessie finishes and hushes, her head still shifting as she waits for the next faithful tourists to gather. I'm befuddled by this cow, and by the introduction she provides to the life and ministry of the world's most celebrated preacher—although, given that the Library was designed in part by entertainment consultants who once worked for Disney, I shouldn't be. Maybe the BGEA thought that Bessie would appeal to kids, though a talking Holstein probably won't hold the interest of any twenty-first-century child older than Billy when he moved into the Homeplace. (And aren't most of the Library's visitors Christian adults?)

But here's what really floors me: Bessie's words seem to be spoken by an African-American woman.

Does this choice of voice strike anybody else as weird, here in this mighty white shrine, especially given the South's vexed racial past? The lively delivery makes it sound like this actress is enjoying herself—perhaps she appreciated the irony or tone-deaf cluelessness of the casting—but still, what a peculiar beginning.

+

From this "lifelike display of a dairy farm," we proceed to brief video testimonies from people whose lives were a mess before they accepted Jesus. They describe their pre-conversion selves in matter-of-fact detail, and we are told that they will complete their testimonies later in the tour. The guides lead us toward a couple of doors that swing open on their own, then we file into the next room, the doors silently shutting behind us as another video starts. I am not pleased about being sealed into a room and forced to watch something until the doors open themselves and the guides herd us cattle to the next station. Nobody else seems bothered, but I have the same feeling that comes on right before an asthma attack: a constriction, an inward clouding, a pressure beginning to build in my tightening chest.

This place troubles me—the underground hymns, the house, and pretty much everything about "the Barn" so far. It doesn't seem a worthy tribute to Graham himself: whatever you think of his message and the way it was delivered, at his best he possessed a sincerity and decency and nuanced intelligence that's missing here. The contrived experience of the Billy Graham Library so far feels more like a flattened-out cartoon than a subtly evocative portrait. Is this the way Billy really was?

+

By this time, we are leaving the Barn proper and moving into the Library's more generic exhibition areas, whose nearly 40,000 square feet tell the story of Billy Graham's life and work, "One Man's Journey." And I confess: I do not treat the subsequent displays and projections with the same care as my wife and her brother and mother, moving much more deliberately behind me. Though only ten or so minutes into the unfolding show, I find myself skimming the rooms and looking for facts or artifacts that might make me and my breathing feel less trapped.

I later read that the Library is meant to be "a place of preserved history, learning, and inspiration"—i.e., a museum, a school, and a church. Can one place manage to be all three? And I read that the mostly self-guided tour is designed to appeal to "casual visitors, spiritual searchers, researchers, historians, and schoolchildren." That is, to put it mildly, an extremely wide range of guests. Again, can one tour possibly appeal to all of them? And where in that list is "church groups," vans and buses full of believers, surely a large constituency? And where does that leave me, a not-exactly-casual visitor and not-exactly-spiritual searcher, looking for quirky but significant details?

It leaves me at the edge of the crowd, in the corner of the room, taking notes in my Moleskine.

+

Billy Graham was converted by a Reverend Mordecai Ham.

+

My wife catches up with me to point out a charming detail in the teen Billy's life, saying (accurately) that it's like something I would have done: in the endpapers of a textbook, he had penciled

Billy Graham

+

~~Libby Cox~~
+
~~Pauline Johnson~~

+

Jean Elliott

with the middle two girlfriends recorded but firmly canceled, as the lover boy with a killer grin moved on.

When Billy was a young man, even once he became a popular preacher, there was a singular intensity and sexiness about him.

+

In the early poor days of their marriage, Ruth Bell Graham made tin-can light fixtures and shades for a little extra money.

+

One of Graham's early successes was the Los Angeles Crusade of 1949, held over for eight weeks in the "Canvas Cathedral"—a big tent meeting, glorified by alliteration. Two of the featured guests at that revival were gospel singers with the names Rose Arzoomanian and Wilmos Csehy. It's hard to accuse Billy of being an ethnocentric American, much less a provincial southerner, especially once he started traveling the globe to spread the gospel, no longer a "country farm boy from Carolina" (if he ever really was) but a citizen of the world.

+

Everyone at the Library is relentlessly friendly—the lady in the Homeplace, the doorman at the foot of the entrance cross, the corny gent at the info desk, the guides strategically placed along the tour. They may be that way by nature, but a chance to minister and witness to visitors must be part of their motivation as Library volunteers. Do they keep an eye out for the possible wayward soul (like, say, a middle-aged guy with longish graying hair who stays at the margins of the group and keeps scribbling in a little black book) and hope—no, pray—that the cheerful performance of their duties and the powerful unfolding of Billy Graham's life and message might lead this poor, lost person to accept Jesus Christ as his personal Lord and Savior?

I'm not poking fun at the faithful. I know that world from the inside: I was raised in a Southern Baptist church, I got saved, I was baptized, I actually attended a Billy Graham Crusade at N.C. State's football stadium in September 1973, with a friend who later became a missionary and has spent most of his adult life living and working as an agronomist in south Asia. But something about the smiling Library staff unsettles me, in the same way that the earnest hymn loops and the big glass cross make me uneasy.

+

I'm fascinated by the "Biblegraph," a "remembrance of the Billy Graham New York Crusade" in 1957. This ingenious arrangement of printed joined cards can be rotated until an arrow points at one of many challenging questions, and the answer appears as a Bible book and chapter and verse in cut-out windows below. *Do you have a "nameless fear"? Do you have moral weakness? Are you harassed by money matters? Are you depressed? Do you have evil thoughts?*

The central feature of this giveaway's design is a cross at the center, not unlike the massive glass cross in the Barn's west wall. But the human scale and tone of this little handheld Biblegraph are much more engaging, much less intimidating.

+

In the photo of Billy Graham with "young gang leaders in East Harlem, New York City"—during that late-fifties New York Crusade—what strikes me is that the local guys are dressed in sports jackets, wearing fedoras and well-polished shoes. They look more like a jazz octet than street toughs.

+

The room demonstrating Graham's use of the media opens with a reproduction of a radio studio and a snippet of an early broadcast. I'm already looking ahead to the exit. But then a primitive TV lights up, and there's Graham on a talk show in the early 1960s, one of several guests—including Woody Allen, back when he was a young comic.

I'm stunned, and I freeze. Billy is finishing up some statement about how "thou shalt not commit immorality," when Woody interrupts that commandment with a wisecrack: "But, um, say you're dating a girl…"

Billy cuts him off, explaining how he wouldn't be doing that because he's married and so on, but Woody has scored his laughs. I really wish I could see the whole exchange, the entire when-worlds-collide show; but no, after a few seconds it's time to turn to the film ministry of the Billy Graham Evangelistic Association and such classics as *The Cross and the Switchblade.*

+

Graham prayed with presidents from Truman forward, and there are lots of displays documenting his interaction with world leaders. He seemed especially involved with Nixon, who may have needed more help than other chief executives: Tricky Dick once borrowed a few bucks from Billy to put in the collection plate, later paying him back. Why am I not surprised?

Some of these interactions were personal and moving: during the Vietnam War, for example, LBJ would ask Graham to come pray with him in the middle of the night. But other official inter-minglings of church and state seem more troubling, like this citation for the Presidential Medal of Freedom, presented by Reagan in 1983: "Reverend Graham's untiring evangelism has spread the word of God to every corner of the globe, and made him one of the most inspirational leaders of the twentieth century. As a deeply commit-ted Christian, his challenge to accept Jesus Christ has lifted the hearts, assuaged the sorrows, and renewed the hopes of millions..." That doesn't seem like language that should be coming from the mouth of the head of the United States government.

+

Though I move quickly through the displays, only lingering when something curious catches my eye, I begin feeling over-whelmed again after an hour or so. Trying to slip out, I find myself at the end of the tour, in the final room about to be sealed for the concluding video testimonies and "seven-minute message from Reverend Graham." I ask the lady guarding the door if I can leave; she says, "Are you sure you don't want to hear the message?" I say, "Yes, very sure"; and so she directs me back out the entrance and down the dark hall to an EMERGENCY EXIT ONLY door. I stand there for a minute, wondering if an alarm will sound when I open this escape hatch for the skeptical or claustrophobic or infirm, with guards converging on the other side to escort me from the Barn as the invisible choir reminds us that *His name is wonderful...*

But no: it's just a door leading into Ruth's Attic, back in the Old Country Store entrance area, where tourists are shopping for t-shirts and videos and religious tchotchkes.

+

And then it hits me: if this is a library, where are the books?

Isn't every library—even a presidential library, a sympathetic, legacy-shaping memorial, which we were told this place is "like"— composed of volumes and documents and papers? Lots of them?

There are copies of The Book throughout the exhibits, but the only actual collection of books at the Billy Graham Library is found here on the shelves of Ruth's Attic, for purchase at the end of the tour—or the beginning, if you choose not to go through the maze representing the phases of Billy's "journey from the pastures and gravel roads of North Carolina."

("Gravel roads"? Was somebody listening to Lucinda Williams and *Car Wheels?* Given all the Piedmont clay hereabouts, "red-dirt roads" would be more like it.)

Surely this word-driven minister had his own library, volumes he liked to have around him in his office as he worked on sermons or columns or his own books. I'd love to see what lined his shelves: reading does shape thinking, after all. Maybe his study has been preserved at The Billy Graham Training Center at The Cove, on the eastern edge of Asheville in the Blue Ridge Mountains, a few hours west of here; or maybe it's to be reproduced somewhere else. But I do wish they'd moved at least some of his books—pages of words that once filled those big hands—to this library.

+

I exit the Barn as I entered, through the foot of the cross.

How dominating it is, this focus of the Library's design. It's the first thing you notice when you drive into the parking lot, and the last thing you see when you look back before heading home. It's the huge dark hinge between outside and in-. You can't escape it.

Which is, I guess, the point; but it makes for some mighty clumsy architecture, like a building I might have designed around the time I was baptized, at age ten, back when I thought I wanted to be an architect. Given Bessie the cow and other features of the Library, it feels like this place is pitched at a fourth-grade level, which may have been exactly what the BGEA wanted for a Christian "family attraction."

But could anything be farther from "the old rugged cross, the emblem of suffering and shame," than this new glossy cross? It symbolizes not agony and humiliation and shameful if atoning death, but power and success and a kind of kitsch, like those glass elevators that architect John Portman started using in his late 1960s hotel designs.

+

Outside, the underground angels are waiting with "Amazing Grace":

When we've been here ten thousand years, bright shining as the sun, we've no less days to sing God's praise than when we first begun.

I begin to relax a little. The muzak's valium is already kicking in.

MICHAEL McFEE   49

+

I sit on a bench in actual October sun, and slowly breathe real air. Billy Graham's beloved Ruth is buried just down the hill, and soon I go visit her grave, set inside a low stone wall filled to the top: it's like a raised planter, a deep bed with space left to one side for her husband, who will be here before too long. Her thick marker—the width and breadth of a coffin, designed to lay on the ground like a lid for the grave—is angled slightly up toward the pilgrim, at about fifteen degrees, with a handsome ideogram at the top (she was raised in China), then her name and dates, and then these words: "End of construction—thank you for your patience."

What an odd postscript and epitaph, an almost jokey or sarcastic punchline, as if concluding the refrigerator-magnet sentiment: "Please be patient—God isn't finished with me yet." When and why did she decide on this? In late 2006, there was a feature in the *Washington Post* about the family's battle over where Ruth and Billy would rest in peace. Toward the end of her life, Ruth dictated "My Final Wishes Concerning My Burial Site," which concluded: "Under no circumstances am I to be buried in Charlotte, North Carolina." But those wishes were changed during her feeble final days, and her son Franklin—the President and Chief Executive Officer of the Billy Graham Evangelistic Association—got what he wanted, which was to have the self-guided tour of the Library conclude at the foot of his famous parents, side by side forever in the Prayer Garden, amen.

+

"Thank you for your testimony this morning," a pinkish man says to a woman as they walk away from Ruth's grave, before rejoining their group to board an Econoway Motor Coach back to Daleville, Indiana.

+

I return to the sunny bench, sit, close my eyes, wait. I'm not praying, but I am mulling and musing. What effect did the Library have on me?

The truth is this: as I proceeded through the exhibits, through "the incredible journey of one simple life," I felt less informed, or instructed, or inspired, than simply sad. Sad for Billy Graham himself, and sorry for his fate. In the beginning, he was a raw, tall, dashing preacher, on fire for the Lord, burning to save souls one by one; then he became the leader of a worldwide evangelistic association, responsible not merely for converting sinners but also for the enormous gospel machinery he'd set into motion; and finally, bent by the weight of all he'd begotten, he became the quiet patriarch with longish white hair, at the mercy of a new generation of believers in a much-changed world. Billy Frank became just another mortal—inevitable, of course, the conclusion to any man's earthly sojourn, but nevertheless melancholy: a dwindling-down, a falling-off, a diminishment. Watching him watch his heir, the somewhat colorless CEO, speaking at the Library's dedication, I thought I saw resignation, if not disappointment, in Graham's blue gaze as he regarded his legacy.

For some reason, Thomas Aquinas comes to mind: looking back over his life and work, the prolific Angelic Doctor and saint said, "It all seems like so much straw."

+

At the cross, at the cross, where I first saw the light, sing the toadstools around me, the melodies and harmonies of their hymn medley never ceasing. *Just as I am, without one plea but that Thy blood was shed for me.* Billy Graham must have heard these words a thousand thousand times during his crusades, during decade after decade of preaching to more than 200 million people; scraps of them must be filling his head now, an elderly widower waiting for the final altar call. *O Lamb of God, I come!*

Tour buses idle in the parking lot. Traffic whooshes by on the interstate beyond the trees, and on the parkway bearing Graham's name. Jets take off and land at the nearby international airport. How many lonely miles did this man travel in his life as the world's pastor, preaching another night in another pulpit, lifting his Bible over his head, wielding the Word?

+

My wife and her brother and mother eventually emerge from the Barn. They found it very interesting, this story of a North Carolina boy who spread the gospel around the world, who was familiar with the powerful and the powerless alike, who was connected to many of the major events and movements of the past half-century; and I agree, he lived an interesting life in a complicated time.

But the Billy Graham Library itself is a disappointing memorial to that influential life, an awkward mix of entertainment, information, and evangelism. It may succeed as a tourist attraction, as another Charlotte theme park, like Carowinds, but I wish it had simply told Graham's life story with the sort of dignity and honesty that the man himself seems to possess. This place may not be "a circus," as Ruth Graham bitterly called it near the end of her life, but with its big-top barn and animal act and "immersive experience with consistent themeing," as the consultant boasted, it's not far off.

I wonder: What does Billy really think of his namesake Library? Not what he might admit in public (if it shares the gospel and saves souls, he'd probably say it was worth it), but what he privately feels about what will be, like it or not, his most public memorial. And what would Jesus—born, according to Luke, in a manger and thus in a stable or a "barn-like structure"—make of all this?

+

At least there's not a lamb of God in the Barn...

As a lapsed Baptist, lapsed choirboy, and lapsed architecture student who became a writer, I know I'm not the Library's ideal visitor. When I first saw that big-cross wall, I thought not *Praise the Lord* but *Uh-oh*. And sure enough, this place's packaging of the evangelist and his gospel message proved too heavy-handed for me.

But I'm pleased that it pleased my mother-in-law. I'm glad that her children could spend this time with their mom, on the first day of her ninth decade in this world. And I'm glad that I came, just as I am, and just as I am not.

+

There's one last structure at the Billy Graham Library, a sort of annex to the second building: a tall concrete silo standing beside the Barn. It's the most striking vertical feature of the campus, though it bears no sign or symbol and its purpose isn't clear: are tourists supposed to visit it, too?

(Later, I discover why the silo looks so unfinished: the plan, as of 2006, was to inscribe the names of big donors on the as-yet-blank concrete. Which means that future visitors will be able to conclude their pilgrimage—before visiting Ruth and Billy flat under their stones, a few steps down the hill—by reading the names of wealthy contributors, preserved in concrete above their heads. What would Jesus have to say about that? Or the young, fiery Billy? Or Ruth herself, forthright to the very end?)

I stroll over to the silo, and around to its back side. A door is cracked there, and I peer inside, hoping to discover some secret before I leave—video surveillance monitors, or a staircase winding up to a prayer loft, or steps descending to those marathon singers locked in the basement, or tons of animatronic silage, singing a song about young Billy Frank...

But no. It's only a room, a dim round space with an ordinary ceiling, a mechanical closet, and a storage place for yard equipment and tools and other stuff humans keep in sheds. What a shame, really. What a waste of a tower, campanile to the Barn's cathedral: I wish there were a working bell in the top, to ring non-electronic notes over the grave of Ruth Bell Graham, playing "It Is Well with My Soul" when the tours are over for the day and the speakers silenced. What a missed opportunity, to get all us mortals a little closer to heaven, if only for a few minutes.

FOR DORIS

It's a pleasure to sing to such a responsive audience.
—The mockingbird, in Randall Jarrell's *The Bat-Poet*

1.

In early April of 2013, I heard that some of Doris Betts's personal library was soon to be sold at the annual Chatham Community Library book sale.

I hadn't been in Pittsboro, North Carolina, since her funeral in the little brick Presbyterian church off the traffic circle, on April 25, 2012. That was a very hard Wednesday morning for those of us who'd known and loved Doris, not just because our friend—one of the most vigorously *alive* human beings in this world—was gone, but also because the Service of Witness to the Resurrection was so impersonal and presbygeneric. Our spirits had *not* been resurrected that day.

I'd been trying to get rid of books in recent years, not buy more; the older I got, the less I liked overflowing shelves of read and unread pages. Too many words, too much dusty paper. But I knew how steadily and how widely and how well Doris always read. I knew this was as close as I'd ever get to seeing my dear friend again, by holding what she'd held and beheld and kept near her for a while.

2.

I heard a lot about the amazing Doris Betts when I was an undergraduate at UNC-Chapel Hill in the mid-1970s; but I was a shy poet and never made my way into her fiction classes or her office.

That means I first made her acquaintance through her books, possibly the best way to meet a writer. Once I read *Beasts of the Southern Wild*, whose short stories astonished and thrilled me, I was a Betts fan.

I can't remember when we first met in person—probably later that decade, during my brief, undistinguished graduate-student career at Carolina—but our connection was immediate and deep. We were both working-class kids from the western part of the state who had transferred to Chapel Hill as juniors and felt like we'd landed in paradise. I was lucky enough to have Doris as my guide and colleague and confidante when I came back to UNC in 1990 as a lecturer in Creative Writing, then (thanks, in large part, to her advocacy) as a tenure-track assistant professor. I watched, and listened, and learned from her example how the department and the university worked, how to take teaching seriously yet continue to write, and above all how to be a public servant at a public university.

This all sounds much more dry than it was. Every minute with Doris sizzled: on the page and in person, she was a force—smart, feisty, hilarious, provocative, tenacious, and fearless. Her fierce dark eyes pierced, sparkled, didn't miss a thing. Nobody was tougher or more tender. She sent the most entertaining e-mails ever, and her notes—written with one of her many fountain pens, held in a hardworking ink-stained hand—were a treasure. I especially loved how she would sometimes sign them: "More to come."

3.

I went to the Chatham library's website to confirm the sale and found a twenty-page list of "special titles" to be offered from the personal collection of Doris Betts. There was plenty of prose, an intriguing range of fiction and non-fiction, but I was mostly interested in poetry, and saw two signed Czeslaw Milosz books. Any poet would cherish those, but they had particular interest for me. He had been a visiting eminence at UNC one semester, and Doris and I and some other writers shared an epic lunch with him in May of 1991, which I remember as The Milosz Monologue—not uninteresting, but totally one-sided. Had he signed those books that day? And his poem "Meaning" (beginning, "When I die, I will see the lining of the world") had been printed in her funeral leaflet, surely at her request, over "In Loving Memory / Doris Waugh Betts / June 4, 1932–April 21, 2012."

But were a couple of poetry books worth the forty-five-minute drive to Pittsboro? I was about to decide No and close the booklist when I saw the item that stopped my scrolling hand, and very nearly my heart:

Jarrell, Randall
illustrations by Maurice Sendak
THE BAT-POET
Macmillan Publishers
inscribed & signed by Jarrell on front endpaper
$20

What? A copy of my favorite book in the world? Not only signed but inscribed (to Doris?) by its author, near the end of his too-short life?

How could I not go?

4.

I don't remember who introduced me to *The Bat-Poet*, but it was truly love at first sight. My wife and I read it aloud to each other, many times; we read it aloud to our young son, many more times; I have given it to who-knows-how-many friends over the years; I have read it to my introductory poetry-writing students, for instruction and sheer pleasure; and it never ceases to delight me.

Why? Because—without ever straining to do so—it satisfies on multiple levels. It's a charming children's book about a bat who, inspired by hearing a mockingbird sing during the day, wants to become a poet, too. (Four of the bat's excellent poems are included.) It's also an instructive adult story about being different from others and discovering one's vocation—in particular, about figuring out how to become a writer. It shows what's involved in realizing one's calling, poem by poem by poem, even if finding an audience is difficult: "The trouble isn't making poems," the bat realizes, "the trouble's finding somebody that will listen to them."

And then, there's the added attraction of "Pictures by Maurice Sendak," as the cover and title page say. Sendak was at the height of his graphic powers in 1964, the year *The Bat-Poet* was published; in fact, he won the Caldecott Medal for his own *Where the Wild Things Are* that year. His atmospheric pen-and-ink drawings for Jarrell's book are marvels of crosshatchery, less illustrations of the scenes than a dreamlike deepening of the text's implications. There are biologically precise details in his rendering of the mockingbird's feathers or the bat's wings or the chipmunk's stripes, but Sendak takes imaginative liberties when needed: the book's one wordless double-page spread—with a lioness and her cub gazing from the scrub-brush shadows—seems to be set in an arid stony landscape far from Guilford County, North Carolina, where the book was written, an hour's drive west of Chapel Hill.

Though he was born in Nashville, Tennessee, and spent much of his professional/professorial life in Greensboro, Jarrell is underappreciated as a Southern writer. That's one reason I particularly enjoy *The Bat-Poet*: it's his most regional book, in its local setting and cast of familiar animal characters. And, apparently, in its composition: in one of her editorial notes for *Randall Jarrell's Letters*, his wife Mary said that in spring 1962 he "stationed himself in a hammock under the pines, among the cardinals and chipmunks, and, with the stereo volume turned up, wrote *The Gingerbread Rabbit* and started on *The Bat-Poet*."

5.

The library sale began on Thursday, April 11, 2013, at 9 A.M.—not the most convenient day and hour, since I had a class to teach at 11 A.M. in Chapel Hill, a good half-hour away. But if I was focused in my book-buying, I could make it to campus in time.

It was a cool, sunny, early spring day, a fine morning for an outing. I left around 8 and took the back way southwest from my home in Durham to the seat of Chatham County, driving through rolling green Piedmont countryside. Doris—who had intensely loved this place and its people—was much on my mind. She'd died almost exactly a year ago, and I still regretted not going to visit her near the end; I hadn't seen her since we had lunch with friends at Fearrington in October 2011.

But on this lovely Thursday, I was thinking about happier times, in particular the lively birthday lunches Doris and I would share every year, a pair of Gemini writers and teachers and Tar Heels born on the same day, June 4th. We'd talk, we'd laugh, we'd drink some wine (her second glass always took the literary gossip to another level), and we'd exchange gifts, usually books—as if either of us needed another volume on our shelves.

6.

I was also wondering: Might Doris actually have known Randall Jarrell?

She was a student at the Woman's College of the University of North Carolina (later UNC-Greensboro) from 1950 to 1952, when he was a celebrated professor there. Did she ever go hear him read, or give a lecture? Did she see him crossing campus, or meet him at some English department function? Did she walk to his office, rap on the door, and announce, "Mr. Jarrell, I'm Doris June Waugh, and I'm a writer, too!"?

Because she already was. Soon she would transfer to Chapel Hill, and her collection of stories *The Gentle Insurrection* would win a national prize for undergraduates and be published by Putnam's in 1954—the year I was born, the year she turned twenty-two—with this italicized pronouncement: "*We, her publishers, believe that Doris Betts possesses one of the most outstanding and unusual writing talents to appear in the past several years, and that the publication of this, her first book, will immediately place her well forward in the ranks of American writers of distinction.*"

7.

"To me, there is no work so dear as teaching.... Teaching is something that I would pay to do; to make my living by doing it, here at the University of North Carolina, with the colleagues I have and the students my colleagues and I have, seems to me a piece of good luck I don't deserve but am immensely grateful for."

Randall Jarrell said this in 1961, upon receiving the Oliver Max Gardner Award for being the outstanding faculty member for the entire UNC system that year. I'm sure that Doris Betts, another devoted and prizewinning professor, would have said exactly the same thing. Both of these writers of distinction were teachers of distinction on their respective campuses—and, really, wherever they went in the state or nation or world: teaching was in their genes.

What made them great teachers? They took their students seriously, they gave thoughtful student writing the close attention it deserved, and they showed those young people how difficult but utterly satisfying it is to be a writer.

Once I asked Doris why some Betts alums had been so successful—books, prizes, literary careers—when others hadn't. She said it wasn't a matter of talent, though a verbal gift or spark was needed to get things going; it was a matter of perseverance, of persistence, of simply not giving up in the face of rejection or indifference. *The trouble isn't making books, the trouble's finding somebody that will listen to them.*

8.

As I approached Pittsboro, I realized that Jarrell had died—slightly less than half a century ago, in Chapel Hill, where he had gone for treatment at the Hand Rehabilitation Center of N.C. Memorial Hospital, after a failed suicide attempt had damaged his left wrist—only twenty-some miles north of where I was driving on the very same road, US 15-501. At 7:30 P.M., on October 14, 1965, walking alone in dark clothes on the shoulder, he was struck and killed by a passing car. The driver said Jarrell "appeared to lunge" into the path of the car, and subsequently many people regarded his death as a suicide; but was it, really? His widow Mary did not think so, and for the rest of her long life defended his reputation against the fate of Plath or Berryman or Sexton, saying that the death certificate's judgment of "accidental" was correct—his sense of balance may have been impaired by medicine he was taking, he may have stumbled on the uneven shoulder and fallen into the road, he was never seriously suicidal, and so on. Who can say?

I wrote a poem about that sad night, in the manner of his famous "The Death of the Ball-Turret Gunner." These five lines don't pretend to solve the mystery, but simply dramatize it:

The Death of Randall Jarrell
Chapel Hill, N.C., 14 October 1965

Was the unsteady man on the shoulder saluting,
or shielding his eyes from the blinding high-beams?
As the passing car sideswiped him, or he the car,
the last thing he saw was his uplifted bare wrist.
Look how the crooked ghost of those stitches gleams.

9

I descended into town, toward the county courthouse (under-going restoration after a devastating fire), and into the traffic circle. As I took the first right and headed west, away from the cemetery behind the church where Doris rested, I remembered that gray day last April, and the little elegy I made shortly afterwards:

Frosted Windows in a Small-Town Presbyterian Church

No stained glass
for instruction or comfort,

just these plain whitened panes,
their blankness

a smothered glow
filling already-numb mourners

with its anesthesia,
as if God's living breath pressed

against each window
from the cemetery just outside

or our own moist exhaled grief
fogged the cool glass,

leaving opaque pages
on which we wish we could write

one last time her beloved name
D O R I S

before the sun erases it,
before it becomes gray stone.

10.

It was only a few blocks to the public library, where a crowd had already gathered—I should have left earlier if I really wanted any of the special titles. I'd brought a bag for my haul; others had brought boxes; the mood was bookish and upbeat.

One of the many retirees in line explained to me, in great detail, how the public library book sale worked in Manhattan; her husband remained silent. I had a nice conversation with a local man and Chatham library volunteer, about Doris and her typically generous work with the library over the years—she lived only a mile or so up the road, on a horse farm outside Pittsboro. He described the mountains of books they removed from her house: having often visited her gloriously messy campus office, I knew that "mountains" was not much of a hyperbole. He told me where the Special Books room was, so that, when the doors opened promptly at 9 A.M., I could hustle there. "That's where the treasures will be," he promised.

11.

By the time I pushed my way through the mob of bibliophiles, a number of books in the "Collector's Corner" had already been plucked from the tables—others had studied that twenty-page inventory as well, and had struck quickly. I looked for the skinny volumes that mean "poetry," and saw the gap where the two Miloszes had been, but no Jarrell. I was disappointed but not surprised, and prepared to consider whatever the dealers and connoisseurs ahead of me in line had left behind.

And then I saw a row labeled "Children's Books"—wait, that's where *The Bat-Poet* should be, right? Was that its narrow brown spine, almost hidden by the big, colorful picture books around it?

Yes. Yes, it was.

12.

I unfroze, pulled the book out, saw the yellow "Signed by Jarrell" slip in it, could not believe my luck. The paperback was a bit worse for wear—one edge looked slightly torn or maybe chewed (Doris always had dogs), and those must have been her coffee stains clouding the sky of Sendak's cover illustration—but I was actually holding the holy-grail *Bat-Poet* in my hands.

It's a pleasure to sing to such a responsive audience.

13.

I retreated a few steps to the corner of that small room, so I could open the book and behold Jarrell's signature in private. I knew what it looked like—modest, undramatic: I'd seen a signed copy of his 1954 novel, *Pictures from an Institution*—but he would have written his name in this copy during the last year he was alive, when he was having the problems that would unfortunately land him in the hand clinic in Chapel Hill, so who knows what it might look like? And what in the world would the inscription be, and to whom?

I confirmed the price on the protruding slip: $20. Though the value of this particular copy of *The Bat-Poet* was hardly the reason I wanted it, I had checked some rare-books websites the previous night. There were only two signed copies available anywhere in the e-world, with this note: "Scarce with Jarrell's signature—$250."

14.

I opened it. I looked. And I laughed.

Here's what was inscribed on the half title page, under what Macmillan had printed there—THE BAT-POET title in capitals, a decorative Sendak sprig or branch, and the author's dedication "to Mary":

and for Doris,
who loves the campus chipmunks—

Happy birthday!

With love and gratitude,
Michael.

4 June 95.

The book was not signed by Jarrell at all, but by me. To Doris.
At one of our birthday lunches.

15.

I could have gotten angry at the library volunteer who somehow mistook my signature and inscription for Randall Jarrell's, and
had caused me to drive so far out of the way on a busy day, wasting
time and gas, and dashing my bibliophiliac hopes. I could have
stomped to the elderly cashier and pitched a hissy fit, demanding—
what? That he acknowledge their error? I could have explained, at
great length, the levels of misunderstanding involved, including,
"How does 'Michael' look like 'Randall,' except for a final 'l'? And
how could Jarrell inscribe a book nearly thirty years after his death?"

But why not just laugh? This whole misadventure seemed
more like a joke than anything else, and I knew that Doris would
have laughed with me at my folly. ("You should be *flattered!*" she'd
tease.) Her laugh was one of the most glorious sounds in the world,
and this mix-up caused me to hear it clearly again. That made the
morning's trip more than worth it.

16

I bought *The Bat-Poet* "signed by Jarrell," though I certainly didn't need another well-used copy, and not at that price. But it pleased me to think of Doris reading that wonderful animal tale about becoming a writer, one set in Jarrell's backyard in Greensboro, a city where Doris had lived before moving to the town of Chapel Hill and becoming the writer and wife and mother and teacher and mentor—self-sacrificing, inexhaustible, inimitable—who meant so much to so many of us. I'd inscribed that book to her at one of our happiest birthday lunches, a few years before her retirement: she'd planned to write the books her multitudinous college duties didn't leave time for, but instead ended up taking care of family members—first her mother, then her husband, then her daughter—during their long final illnesses, before she succumbed to the lung cancer she'd hoped to avoid by stopping smoking decades earlier.

I bought some other overpriced Doris treasures, too. As I drove north from Pittsboro to the university on its hill, I wished I could walk into the English building and hear her voice quickening the halls. I also wished I had a recording, on CD or MP3, of the old Caedmon LP on which Jarrell reads—in a quavery, witty, precise voice—his book beginning, "Once upon a time there was a bat—a little light brown bat, the color of coffee with cream in it."

I slipped a note out of my shirt pocket, which I'd planned to tuck inside the precious signed volume. Doris had slid the card into my departmental mailbox shortly after our birthday lunch in 1995. On it she had stamped *Doris Betts, Professor of English*, with this postscript message written in her spirited pen-and-ink hand:

"Michael—I forgot one other thing in my e-mail—I meant to tell you how much I LOVED *The Bat Poet*!

"doris."

RELIEF

1.

In late August 1986, I was a Tar Heel in exile, and excited about it. I'd just begun my year as poet-in-residence at Cornell, I had a spacious apartment in an old house near campus, and I had time to write every day, a luxury not enjoyed at home in North Carolina. What more could a young poet ask?

The first week in Ithaca was very productive, a writer's dream. The second week was less satisfying, because I'd begun to miss my wife and two-year-old son, nine hours to the south: she would take a leave from her job in January, so that they could come live with me during the wintry "spring" semester, but till then the two of them had to stay back in Durham. The third week was terrible: I missed them so much I couldn't really concentrate on any work. All I did was count the days and hours and minutes till I saw them in the Syracuse airport.

When my little boy came toddling down the ramp from the gates, I called his name and ran toward him and then (much to my surprise) collapsed. My legs gave way. I sank to the dirty tiles. I started crying. I was tearfully overjoyed to see him, to hear and touch and smell him, simply to *be* with him and his mother, my wife, the loves of my life. I had been physically craving their presence, and now the distance was closed—for a few days, at least.

To a less dramatic degree, yet in the same way, that's how I feel about my native place, western North Carolina, in particular south Buncombe County and Asheville and the surrounding terrain. I've lived a full and fortunate life in the Piedmont, 225 miles to the east, for more than four decades, but I've never stopped missing the mountains, longing for them, yearning to return, if only for a little while. I need to migrate there, now and then. My body seems to require elevation, the kind of serious geographical relief you can't get in Durham County, where I live, or Orange County, where I work. No matter how many times I've driven I-40 West, when I get the first clear view of those imbricate blue ranges unfolding ahead of me, at the Dysartsville Road exit between Morganton and Marion, my eyes tear up, my pulse quickens, and I fall silent in gratitude. I feel *relieved*. I'm home.

2.

It was not always thus.

I couldn't wait to leave the mountains, once I approached college age. My childhood and teenhood there were pretty happy, all in all, but I never considered attending an upland university. I wanted to be in a bigger, busier, more worldly place, one not isolated by encircling hills.

Maybe reading *Look Homeward, Angel* at the hormone-addled age of sixteen (perfect timing) planted this seed, or helped water it. But by the time I headed to the School of Design at N.C. State, I was ripe for escape.

3.

I could put the mountains behind me, in the rearview mirror, but I hadn't grasped an unexpected physiological fact: they were somehow *inside* me, deep in my body and mind.

Once in Raleigh, I found myself looking for hills at the horizon, behind all those brick buildings: not there. I found myself listening to the way people talked, and wishing I could hear the pointed Appalachian locutions of my family. (Not that I would have known to call them "Appalachian" at that time; such regional self-consciousness was not part of my education in Buncombe County Schools.) I found myself craving the switchback of a mountain road, the steep climb and fall of a trail, the changes in feet above sea level that I'd taken for granted. As a pithy fellow hillbilly once said, while sojourning in the Piedmont: "Ain't enough vertical element to this."

After I transferred to Chapel Hill in 1974, and signed up for a creative writing class, and got over Trying to Sound Like an English Poet in my poems, and discovered contemporary western North Carolina writers, I found myself going back to the mountains I couldn't put behind me after all, in lines and stanzas, in poem after poem, in elegies for what I'd left behind but still loved. I felt like I gained strength from touching that higher ground, if only in words.

4.

For fun, sometime toward the end of elementary school—grades one through eight, at old Valley Springs School in Skyland, which housed all twelve grades when I started there at age six—I wrote out my complete address:

Mike McFee
160 Locust Court
Royal Pines
Arden
Buncombe County
North Carolina
United States of America
North America
Western Hemisphere
Earth

As the teacher's pet and class egghead, I probably wanted to elaborate on the astronomical location, but I stopped with Earth, fortunately. What did I know, really, about space, or (for that matter) the globe, or the far-flung continent and country and state? What I did know was the first four lines in that strung-out list: our

house, our neighborhood, our town, our county. What I knew—
what rooted and nourished me then, and later as a writer—was the
local: it was my world, if not *the* world, and those places anchored
me.

5.

Locust Court was one of several dozen streets in Royal Pines, a
lower-middle class subdivision clumped along Highways 25 and
25A, midway between Asheville and Hendersonville. Most of the
streets were named for trees. Locust was between Walnut and
Chestnut: it began at Cedar Lane then climbed (over several long
hills—we lived at the top of the first one) across Royal Pines Drive
and past Hemlock Street, ending at Oak Terrace and Hickory
Court, its terminus pointed toward the 2,996-foot summit of
Mount Royal. This may sound sylvan and poetic, but in fact most of
the houses were small and cheaply made, and most of the families
were, like us, working-class at best. There was nothing particularly
distinctive about Royal Pines, no upscale sidewalks or streetlights or
"improvements": it was just streets and lots and people getting by.

That made it a great place to be a kid. From an early age, I
could, and did, simply *roam*. On foot, on bike, by myself or with my
dog, I'd visit friends' houses, I'd look for a pickup game to join, I'd
explore the vacant lots or undeveloped woods. I'd head out the door
and be gone all day, and—in that earlier, safer, less paranoid time—
nobody worried about it. I waged hot dirt-clod and crabapple wars
with my buddies, I played kick-the-can at dusk with the kissable
girls, I used my imagination and my wits and, once or twice, my
fists.

The adults could be pretty interesting. One neighbor was a
shell-shocked World War II veteran who would utter wildly inappropriate profanities or sexual remarks, then immediately forget
them. One was a hard-living woman whose sons loved Richard Pet-
ty more than God, and kept a blue #43 Plymouth in the yard. One

was a genteel man from Florida who lived with his Cadillac-driving ancient mother: after their boxer dogs attacked and disfigured the next-door-neighbor girl, he destroyed them and we rarely saw him outside again.

Have I written about all this? You bet. My street gave me place, images, character, story, *relief.* There was nothing flat about the place, metaphorically or literally: you were always going up or down, even walking to the mailbox or your beat-up car. Locust Court has a cameo in the first poem in my mercifully-out-of-print first book, which offers "Directions" to an idealized location in the mountains: "the sunken asphalt / patch that looks like Africa" was right in front of our house, one of many ineffectual repairs on the cracked concrete streets of hilly Royal Pines.

6.

There was nothing regal about the Royal Pines of my youth, and many of the tall evergreens had been cut down. (My sarcastic best friend said it should be called "Royal Stumps.") I was painfully aware of how much less grand it was than, say, Oak Forest, an affluent development close to the high school where all the cutest girls and coolest guys seemed to live, in huge brick houses with finished basements and lush green yards.

But mediocrity was not the original plan for our neighborhood.

A two-page spread in the Asheville *Times* of Sunday, May 31, 1925, announced "the Formal Opening of Beautiful Royal Pines," whose handsome logo—a stylized pine flanked by a capital R and P, set inside a crown—proclaimed it "Asheville's Suburb Supreme." "Thursday," the ad proclaimed, "on the Dixie Highway, between the resort cities of Asheville and Hendersonville, Royal Pines will be the scene of unusual interest as thousands will be introduced to the Many Wonderful Features of this Superb Estate which has been in the process of development for nearly 100 years and is positively peerless in its Rare Beauty." Across the tops of the pages were "A

Photographic Reproduction of the Beautiful Painting, 8 x 20 feet, executed by L. Francis—the largest in North Carolina—portraying Asheville, Kenilworth, Biltmore, and Royal Pines," and an "Interesting Drawing Showing the Location of Royal Pines with Relation to Asheville and Other Points on the Dixie Highway," including the Biltmore House and the Biltmore Forest Country Club and Golf Course.

Which is to say: The developer of Royal Pines, the William I. Phillips Company, was aiming pretty high, or at least associating this new development with the classier parts of Asheville. "Here, on a delightful elevation of 2,300 to 2,600 feet, with a magnificent view of Mt. Pisgah and several mountain ranges, will be erected many fine homes, since practically every lot is amply large enough to permit the building of a pretentious home." All this overheated copy—with its pretentious use of "pretentious" and Important Capital Letters—was intended not for western North Carolinians but for rich folks from Florida or New York, looking to invest their money in a summer home, a scaled-down version of George Vanderbilt's chateau but "fine" nonetheless. There was even going to be a Royal Pines Casino, "a magnificent structure—with a large swimming pool, a dance floor, locker room, and a grandstand—destined to be the center of Asheville's social life throughout the entire summer season."

What went wrong? Despite the real-estate hype, most lots were barely half an acre, puny by the standards of Biltmore Forest, the genuinely posh suburb that Vanderbilt's widow Cornelia began developing on Estate land earlier in the 1920s. Royal Pines was hardly a century old or "peerless in its Rare Beauty": its residents did not enjoy "magnificent mountain views," much less the promised "planted parkways" and other "high-class development" amenities.

But the real problem was the stock market crash of 1929, three years later, when Royal Pines was still struggling to get off the ground. Nobody had money to invest, and the suburb never really got developed in a supreme manner, despite the alliterative effort.

When lots and houses finally did get sold—like, say, Lot 16 on Block 16, a.k.a. 160 Locust Court, in August 1947—the purchasers were not wealthy Miamians looking for a seasonal cottage, but hardscrabble locals like my just-married parents, buying a small house and lot they could make into a respectable suburban place over the coming decades.

Did I know any of this local history growing up? No. And my folks didn't tell me, if they knew. But in the layout of the streets, in a few of the original houses, in the very name itself, Royal Pines, there was always the hint of something grander having almost happened there. Which is the sweet spot for a writer.

7.

Arden, the next ring on my elementary address bulls-eye, didn't exactly exist. As the *North Carolina Gazetteer* drolly notes: "Incorporated 1883, but long inactive in municipal affairs." Unlike Biltmore Forest, there was no town, no town hall, no sense of Arden as a civic unit. It was a not-so-wide place on the road, just north of the Henderson County line: when I was growing up, if you drove less than a mile in any direction, there was nothing but deep darkness and stars out there at night.

The *Gazetteer* continues: "Known first as Shufordsville. Renamed Arden for the Forest of Arden in Shakespeare's *As You Like It*." As with Royal Pines, the name Arden manifested higher aspirations: rather than simply name your place for the most prolific clan in the area, why not go for something finer, exclusive-sounding, dramatically sylvan? And as with Royal Pines, the reality fell short of the dream.

The *Gazetteer* concludes: "Alt. 2,225." The elevation at our Locust Court address, according to the Buncombe County Online Slope Calculation Tool, is 2,340 feet, roughly 2,000 feet higher than the house where I now live in Durham. I grew up at elevation. Life there always involved verticality, going higher or lower, not merely continuing out and out and out, as in the flatlands. Though I couldn't see Pisgah's peak (alt. 5,271) from my yard, it was looming at the horizon, waiting for me to come to a clearing and spy it in the distance, crowning the ridge to the southwest, one of many dozens of mountains whose relief was a darker blue border always grounding the sky.

8.

Asheville itself wasn't part of my youthful address, because I didn't actually reside there; but it was, and is, very much a part of my life.

Granny McFee lived—with various female kin: all the men were gone—at 76 Arlington, a few blocks off Charlotte Street, at the other end of that thoroughfare from the high-tone Grove Park Inn neighborhood. Hers was a skinny clapboard house with a second floor (intriguing to me: no upper stories in Royal Pines) and a root cellar under the side porch, that spooky pit where she kept her many canned goods. I can close my eyes and still see every room. When I opened the front door, vivid smells greeted me, mostly from her cooking—my grandmother's Thanksgiving meal was truly a heavenly feast—but also from her arthritis and asthma remedies. She and her sisters and daughters doted on me, and I did not resist. I was not allowed to roam, since Asheville was the Big City and therefore dangerous, but if they'd let me, I would've gone out the front door and turned right, up the steep hill, and tromped onto Beaucatcher Mountain (alt. 2,694), just as I wandered around Mount Royal out in the county.

Asheville offered urban pleasures, though. My mother took my sister and me to Pack Memorial Library, back when it was actually on Pack Square. How exotic, the child-scale wooden Indian inside the entrance! How exciting, being allowed to touch and read and check out so many books! She also took us to the S&W Cafeteria on Patton Avenue, that stylish Deco building: how adult I felt there, eating my cherry pie, fetching fresh coffee for Mom as she smoked her after-dinner cigarette. And she hauled us into town to attend First Baptist Church, that elegant domed place of worship. We could've gone to Arden Baptist Church, not a mile from our house in Royal Pines, but Mom—a social dreamer if not an actual social climber, who adored the Biltmore House and the S&W and First Baptist, monuments to loftier cultural possibilities—wanted us to worship with the most refined Southern Baptists in the area.

Have I written about all this? Oh yes. The Asheville that I knew growing up—where my beloved grandmother and aunts lived, where we ate out and bought clothes, where we went to church and the library and the movies—is not the groovy Asheville of today, with its hipster kids and wealthy retirees, its ever-expanding beer and food and arts culture. Back then, the new mall was draining downtown of its businesses, and the still-mired-in-Depression-debt city had a somewhat abandoned feel. But I loved going there, and simply walking its hilly blocks, and still do. It's personal: there's the old post office where my father worked the graveyard shift, there's the Grove Arcade where my mother processed foreign meteorological data for the government, there's where several aunts were salesladies at Bon Marché department store, there's Tops for Shoes where my sister and I got our feet x-rayed, there's the Flat Iron Building where we went to the dentist. And there's where I—a naïve, seventeen-year-old would-be literary scholar, preparing to write his senior thesis on James Joyce—bought a copy of *Ulysses* at Talman's, on Pritchard Park: the wry bookseller, a tall man, looked down at me over his glasses and said, "You think you're ready for this, pal?"

9.

Sometimes when I'm back in Asheville, I'll visit my parents. They're buried in the Rest Haven section of Green Hill Cemetery west of downtown, across the French Broad River, off busy Patton

Avenue. Mom and Dad are side by side, near the topmost point in the graveyard, with a fine view of Mount Pisgah to the southwest, on a clear day. I'll clean off their flat stones, maybe put some nice artificial flowers in the sunken pots, and tell them the most recent family news.

From 1958 to 1962, they bought four plots on the installment plan: one for each of them, one for their daughter, and one for their son. My estranged sister died in 2006, at the age of 54, and her ashes were scattered somewhere along the parkway by her companion of many years—I don't know where. Her space will never be used, not by her. Though I like the idea of enjoying a prospect of Pisgah for eternity, I won't use the space waiting for me either: my own family and homeplace are elsewhere now. I think I'll leave that plot, that narrow little lot, undeveloped.

10.

My firsthand knowledge of Buncombe County, the last local item in my address list, was selective, focused on and around the Blue Ridge Parkway, that most sublime of tourist roads: it loops into Buncombe County from the northeast, curving past Craggy Gardens and down toward Asheville but then swooping south of the city, between it and Arden, before climbing back up into the national forest to Mount Pisgah and the Haywood County line. That's a lot of picturesque blacktop, and my family liked to take Sunday-afternoon drives along the parkway: it was, or at least felt like, free entertainment when gas was thirty cents a gallon or less, to glide on that two-lane highway above the valley where we spent the rest of the week, looking down on the world and out at the sweet bluegreen view, passing through tunnels and sometimes disappearing into fog or clouds but always emerging on the other side, in the clear, nearly a mile high in the sky.

Such prospects, such perspective, stirred the young poet in me. In fact, the first poem in my senior creative writing thesis at UNC, called "Overlook," was about pulling off the parkway and savoring the view. But that came years later. When I was a teenager, especially once I learned to drive, the Blue Ridge Parkway was about two things.

One was romance. I liked to take prospective girlfriends on a slow ride up that road whose mountain prospects rendered conversation unnecessary, parking the car at a remote overlook then hiking to a more secluded spot where we could recline on a blanket and enjoy a picnic and, I hoped, each other. There was something about canoodling in the open air, at 4,000 feet, that felt practically Edenic, the two of us isolated in a high green garden with a long blue view, flushed and happy.

But such occasions were, believe me, rare. Mostly, the parkway was about hiking and camping, on my own or with friends. Many remarkable trails began at or crossed over that road, and I took lots of them across ridges, up to peaks, down to secluded valleys: those walks were excellent lessons in staying alert, in using every sense to experience the world around me as carefully and fully as possible. Now and then, a buddy and I would hike deeper into the national forest, pitch our tent by a creek or river, cook up dinner over a Coleman stove, and sleep out in the woods with the other animals. I'll never forget waking one March morning, near John Rock, to absolute silence and stillness, and a canvas roof sagging inches from my face: out of nowhere, it had snowed several feet overnight. For hours, we made our weighty way through holy dazzle back to the car, without seeing or hearing another human being. It was glorious.

11.

Did growing up in the mountains predispose me to be a poet?

Probably not. And yet, the daily vertical movement of living at higher altitudes is not unlike the experience of writing a poem, which doesn't so much cross the page as descend it, in a kind of back-and-forth dance. The turn at the end of each line is not unlike the turn at a switchback, reversing to where you came from but a bit lower, making progress toward a desired but unpredictable destination, your load lightening somehow. Paying close attention on steep trails and roads is not unlike stepping deliberately along the poetic line, sustaining your rhythm and momentum just so, not too fast but not too slow, focusing on the details underfoot and at hand while also appreciating the long view, if you lift your eyes to the horizon.

Of course, "not unlike" is not "like." And yet, it's close. It's kin.

12.

Two mountain prospects hang on the wall in my home office.

Number 1: A 16 x 21-inch black-and-white print, "1891. Bird's-Eye View of the City of Asheville, North Carolina"—a reproduction of the original, issued by Bon Marché in August 1947, the month my parents married and bought the Royal Pines property. The little county seat ("Population 1880, 2,610; 1890, 11,500") looks like a wilderness town, with the forest creeping in from the west, and with not that many buildings clustered on its streets—the 1876 courthouse on the square, the churches on Church Street, and the original Battery Park Hotel on Haywood, from whose porch George Vanderbilt first saw Pisgah, twenty miles away to the south, a mountain he would later own, as well as all the valley between him and that peak. Most of the named structures on this view are long gone, e.g., the huge Asheville Furniture Manufactory by the flood-prone French Broad, running along the bottom of the print. What's still there is the landscape, the underlying topography, the bones that the modern city's flesh covers: the flats by the river, "Vally" Street (the African-American part of town) clearly in a valley below Market Street hill, the shadow-casting ridges rising up and climbing to the north/south path of Main Street, the undeveloped acclivity of Beaucatcher disappearing beyond the top of the print. Arlington

Street is not labeled, but I see the beginning of its first block, and—with my magnifying glass—I can guess where my grandmother's house will soon be built, where my father's family will situate itself, near the foot of that in-town mountain.

Number 2: A Transverse Mercator Projection of the Knoxville quadrant (NI 17-1) of the U.S. Geological Survey—i.e., a 20 x 31-inch plastic representation of the mountains from Marion, North Carolina, to east Tennessee, the elevation contours rendered in 3-D relief, so that the scale-model ridges and peaks rise up like actual ridges and peaks from the plain of the sheet. Unlike the 1891 Bird's-Eye View, which is after all a fanciful elaboration of a city map, filled out with non-existent individual trees and generic structures, this Mercator Projection NI 17-1 bristles with accurate data, as you might expect from something prepared by the Defense Mapping Agency Topographic Center: numbered roads, named towns and bodies of water and mountains, railroads and county lines, longitude and latitude. Asheville is a sprawling yellow blob in the valley interrupting Pisgah National Forest, and Royal Pines is a speck on the Skyland/Arden drip from that blob.

This map has brought me many hours of pleasure. I can study it on the wall, running my fingers along the crest-hugging Blue Ridge Parkway, touching the top of Mount Royal in Arden, following the flow of the Davidson River past John Rock. I can find unmarked Max Patch (4,629 feet), where my mother spent World War II handling accounts at a lumber mill, way out in the wild Great Smoky Mountains on the NC/TN state line. I can lay the projection flat on a table, and kneel till my eye is at map-level, or I can lay it on the floor and look down as if from a great height: either way, the rumpled, complicated landscape of home is there, spread out before or below me, and for a few seconds—squinting—I can pretend that I'm actually seeing it. That cartographic comfort has helped me through some cold homesick times in Ithaca, in Appleton, and even in Durham, when my eyes and heart and imagination needed a little relief.

13.

The first poem in my first book was set in the mountains, and so is the last poem in my fourteenth book, a 27-part sequence called "McCormick Field," set in and around the baseball park in Asheville where my father and I spent our closest times together.

Mountainous poems framed my poetry-publishing career, in 2012. That made me wonder: How many of the poems in my books were actually set in Buncombe County or western North Carolina, or dealt with family characters and stories from there, or somehow involve that Appalachian part of the world?

The tally, including my most recent collection *We Were Once Here* (2017):

My eight full-length "regular" poetry collections contain 275 poems total. Of those, 134—almost exactly half—deal with mountain material, in whole or in part.

In particular: ten of the thirty poems in my first book had to do with Appalachia; nineteen of twenty-three in the second; twenty-two of twenty-two in the third, wholly based on the life of my mother; and then, thirteen of forty-one, eighteen of thirty-nine, seventeen of thirty-seven, seventeen of thirty-one, and eighteen of fifty-two.

At first, I was shocked at those high percentages, especially since I haven't lived in the Blue Ridge for more than forty years. But the more I thought about it, the less I was surprised: "When I need inspiration," as I said in an interview years ago, "I automatically go back to the mountains in my writing." They seem to be my given subject matter, my default mode as a writer. Living at a distance from the hills has provided a helpful clarifying perspective, and sharpened the yearning to return in poems and essays.

And I don't seem to be done yet. One of the poetry books I've been working on for a while is about the early years of Biltmore, from 1888—when Vanderbilt conceived the idea of buying land south of Asheville and building a grand chateau, the biggest private home in America—into the very early twentieth century. What got me going on this project was wondering: What happened to the mountain people who were actually living on those hundreds of thousands of acres that the richest bachelor in the world bought? What effect did that millionaire's ambition have on the locals, in one of the poorest corners of the country? Were any ancestral McFees displaced by the Vanderbilts?

One day I may stop mining the mountain vein. But I doubt it. I don't think I want to. I don't think I can.

THE MAIL

1.

I confess: I'm obsessed with the mail. Maybe it's familial—after all, my father was a postal worker for more than three decades. Maybe it's occupational: as a writer, many rejections and some acceptances and a few fitful checks for work published have come to my mailbox, a personal terminal for departures and arrivals. Or maybe it's temperamental, a matter of preference and habit. I like writing on paper, I like reading on paper, I like unfolding paper and holding it in my hands, I like exchanging written-on and folded-up paper with friends far away for less than two quarters, I like rereading what they've taken the time and effort to send me, and I like thinking that they may do the same thing with the mail I've sent them.

2.

"Consider paperless billing," invites my power company, on the unstamped return envelope. "It's simple. It's convenient. It's safe."

I know it is. I know I probably should—in fact, I do direct billing for a few monthly fees already. I know that, before long, I'll be paying for everything by paperless charge.

But I just can't go all in, not yet. Why? Not because I distrust the adjective "paperless," though (as a writer of a certain vintage) I do, but because I want to keep giving business to the United States Postal Service.

I write a dozen or so checks around the first of each month, I slip those signed rectangles into the envelopes whose flaps I lick and seal, and I affix attractive self-adhesive postage stamps purchased at my local post office. Later in the day, out running errands, I drive that stack of drafts to the P.O., roll up to a big blue collection (a.k.a. "snorkel") box, roll down my window, and slip the envelopes into its slot, listening as they slide to a muffled landing on other dropped-off paper below.

A public USPS mailbox comforts me. I appreciate its shape, a mass-produced barrel vault, a truncated metal tunnel. I appreciate its squeaky lowered drawer, whose loud swinging shut confirms, *Your mail is safe in here.* I appreciate something that's so accessible and yet so private, its contents reachable only by a postal employee with a key, kneeling or squatting to empty the mail into a tray he hauls away so other postal employees can begin the processing of its contents. It dismays me that many thousands of these boxes—these outward and visible symbols of our democratic interconnectedness: touch any one of these nodes and you've touched the entire neuropostal network of America—were removed after the terrorist and anthrax attacks of September 2001. I wish I owned one, to secure my decades of correspondence (or myself, in blue moods) inside its cryptlike chamber, but I'll have to settle for the beat-up green U.S. Mail coin bank on my desk, a meticulous reproduction that accepts change rather than letters in its slot. It even has a tiny framed space for posting pick-up times, the promised hour and minute of return, the first step toward delivery.

3.

On a recent trip to Scotland, I took two photos of Royal Mail public posting boxes. One was barely larger than a shoebox turned up on its end, set flush into a stone wall in Jedburgh: the crown at the top, framed by a V and an R, meant that it had been in this spot since Victoria was queen—well over a century. The first time it was painted red, horses would have clopped up the hilly street it faced. The key made for its hole would have looked like something out of

Dickens. I entrusted the box's narrow slot with a postcard that took weeks to get back to the States, a stately pace that didn't bother me at all, since I was thus at home to receive my own message from the homeland.

The other was a freestanding red pillar box in Oban, a tall, cast-iron Victorian cylinder with a dentate cap. It looked like a colossal fire hydrant there on the esplanade, and it cheered me greatly, that postal sentinel (slightly rusted at its base by salty spray) looking across the bay toward the Western Isles, toward remote Colonsay where the MacPhies lived for many centuries before heading west to Ireland then across the Atlantic to America and southwest into Appalachia, before one of them, my father, William Howard McFee, returned to North Carolina from a European war and began to realize that what a foot soldier like him really wanted was a good, steady, unperilous job at the post office.

4.

During my 1974 study-abroad term in Oxford, I loved writing back to the States—postcards, stamped with the queen, and also lightweight letters sealed into flimsy Air Mail envelopes, diagonally striped blue and red at the edges. I'd scrawl *PAR AVION* across the front and back, as if that weren't already clear, or as if I actually knew French.

But the most entertaining way to write home was via aerogram, those thin blue sheets that are both letter and envelope. I'd never seen such postal ingenuity. After writing my missive on the blank side, I'd fold the bottom up and the top down, then seal the two side flaps and top flap, then address the already-stamped *aerogramme* and drop it into the closest Royal Mail box, feeling *très international*.

5.

Our mailwoman in the boxy white USPS truck, with its big blue speeding-eagle-head logo, services each odd-numbered box on the far side of the road—pulling over, stopping, lowering the mailbox door, delivering, closing it firmly, and driving on—before she reverses course and visits the even boxes on this side of the road. In the few minutes before she comes back, I pretend to keep working here at my writing desk, but what I'm really doing is waiting for the sound of her approaching to my left, the sound of her stopping in front of the house next door, and the sound of her mild acceleration to my oversized mailbox, sometimes with its red semaphore arm raised to signify outgoing mail laid inside, a little something to balance the ongoing exchange of posted paper.

Like a bus driver, pulling over and pulling away, again and again, the mailwoman has a route, a routine, one she follows every weekday, usually arriving right around lunchtime.

I have a routine, too, once she's gone. It could be called The 100 Steps. Steps 1–3: Leave my office. Steps 4–6: Walk to the front door, unlock and open it. Steps 7–11: Cross the front porch, our heavy old screen door clapping shut behind me. Steps 12–15: Step down onto the sidewalk for a few paces, pausing by the sprawling rosemary bush, which I pinch for postal good luck. Steps 16–22: Turn hard right and cross the grassy plateau in front of the azaleas; sniff aromatic fingers; feel herbal and hopeful. Steps 23–43: Cross the shallow valley of the front yard, up the slope to a narrow passage between quince bush and ash tree. Steps 44–54: Circle around to the front of the gray box; open door, peer in, retrieve mail, close box up till tomorrow. Steps 55–91: Walk back across the yard, a deliberate passage that allows for preliminary review of promising mail. Steps 92–100: Back to sidewalk, across porch; open door, slip shoes off: route completed, mail truly delivered, ready for scrutiny.

Such a description sounds much more obsessive-compulsive than it is; I've never actually counted the steps until today. But the pattern, the manner of retrieval, is pretty much the same, whenever I'm at home, rain or shine, and has been for the decades we've lived in this house.

6.

Here's another way to describe The 100 Steps:

Pilgrimage

Six days a week, this solo pilgrimage
across the wilderness
                    of weedy sloughs
and uphill root-snares and dead-lightning limbs
to the mailbox,
                    celestial castle on the hill,
a shining silver roadside barrel vault
with a bloody flag
                    recently lowered
and a drawbridge I let down while lifting out
my daily bread,
                    the world's delivered words
I bear back to the house along a path
my feet have carved
                    into the local earth
for decades now and know so well they could
tightrope its shallow gulley in the dark.

I wrote that poem four years ago, apparently in a medieval metaphorical mood. Today, it seems overwrought to me, though I freely admit to holy feelings about the mail. Even on an off day—no letters or cards, just bills or junk—home delivery seems like a local miracle, a visit from one of a host of unionized courier angels whose continuing existence and presence say, *Fear not, I bring you good tid-*

ings. And at the very least, those tidings are *Somebody knows you're still here,* which, especially as I age, is no small comfort.

7.

On a recent postal holiday—a Monday when my wife pointedly reminded me, at breakfast, "Don't forget, there won't be any mail today"—I nevertheless walked to the box as usual, to check on whether anything had come yet. *D'oh!* I said, slamming the door shut.

When I checked the empty box again, a few hours later, I laughed and shook my head. The Absent-Minded Professor at Home!

The third and last forgetful time I made my pointless pilgrimage, I thought, *I may have a problem here.*

8.

The postman—that intermediary between us and the big indifferent world out there—is a recurrent figure in popular culture. "Please Mister Postman," beg the Marvelettes, and later John Lennon in the Beatles cover version I knew, switching the genders involved, asking the carrier to look and see if there's a long-awaited card or letter from his girlfriend, saying she's coming back home. What fruitful tension, lovers apart and (maybe) trying to stay in touch: a number of other songs also involve letters and the man delivering (or not delivering) them.

Movies, too. *Il Postino*—a film based on Antonio Skármeta's novel *Neruda's Postman*—was a hit in the mid-1990s. I recently rewatched it, trying to remember why it was popular, but all I could think was: If I have to be exiled from my country, can it please be to somewhere like the Capri hilltop villa in this movie, where the elderly poet lives with his beautiful wife and spectacular mountain views, and a simple villager is hired exclusively to deliver my daily mountains of mail, including correspondence from the Nobel Committee in Sweden?

Don Pablo is more patient with his aspiring-writer carrier than I would be, talking with him about poetry, loaning him books, helping him woo gorgeous Beatrice Russo—though her overprotective mother is suspicious: "When a man starts to touch you with words," she says to Neruda, "he's not far off with his hands.... He's heated her up like an oven with his metaphors!" I doubt this film adds much to our understanding of the Chilean poet, or of Communism, or of simple rural postal workers in early 1950s Italy, but it's an entertaining movie for the first hour or so. And it nicely captures a writer's dependence on the mail, his connection to others so far away.

I have a reproduction of Mary Cassatt's 1891 print *The Letter* taped to the lid of my envelope-box: I love how the pensive woman appears to be eating the unaddressed envelope, though she's only lifted it to her lips to lick its flap. But my favorite piece of postal-based art may be Van Gogh's *Postbode Roulin*, an 1889 portrait, one of at least a dozen paintings of Roulin family members. The mailman is posed against bright green floral wallpaper, wearing a blue POSTES hat and double-breasted blue peacoat, staring at us with unearthly blue eyes. His expression is wonderfully enigmatic, eyebrows slightly raised and lips lightly pursed, as if Roulin is bemused by this artist who wants to paint a picture of him in uniform. The best part of this painting is his beard, a fabulous swirling cloud of curls so full and long that he must part it to either side of his chest, exposing a bit of the base of his throat. I like that flowing facial hair much more than the starry starry night Van Gogh painted the following summer: it's divine, and so is Roulin, an impressionist God the Father of all postmen. I keep a postcard of *Postbode Roulin* in my home office: he watches my back as I write, waiting for me to send more words through the mail.

Eudora Welty's famous "Why I Live at the P.O." isn't really about the post office, except as a place where the narrator-postmistress moves to escape her nutty Mississippi family. I do like her defense of reading the postcards she handles—"If people want to write their inmost secrets on penny postcards, there's nothing in the wide world you can do about it, Uncle Rondo"—and her understanding of the central social role of the P.O. in an early twentieth-century small town: "There are always people who will quit buying stamps just to get on the right side of Papa-Daddy."

Speaking of writers, and Mississippi, and stamps, William Faulkner served three desultory years as postmaster at the University of Mississippi. He resigned in October 1924, writing: "As long as I live under the capitalistic system, I expect to have my life influenced by the demands of moneyed people. But I will be damned if I propose to be at the beck and call of every itinerant scoundrel who has two cents to invest in a postage stamp." That's a grandly literary way of going postal.

10.

In pre-electronic-transmission days, most writers not employed by the postal service were fairly hawkish about mail service: they counted on it to take their words where they needed to go, and to bring them back again. As Randall Jarrell wrote, in a letter, "The mailman is every writer's tutelary deity."

Jarrell's colleague at UNC-Greensboro, Robert Watson, wrote my favorite poem about the mail, "Please Write: Don't Phone," first published in the late 1970s. "While there is mail, there is hope," it begins, a decidedly old-fashioned pronouncement, then contrasts a letter with a phone call: "After we have hung up, I can't recall / Your words, and your voice sounds strange / Whether from distance, a bad cold, deceit / I don't know." Watson's case for handwritten correspondence seems especially poignant now, in these days of e-mail and texting and ever swifter or hipper ways to communicate. "Let us write instead," he urges: "surely our fingers spread out / With pen on paper touch more of the mind's flesh / Than the sound waves moving from throat to lips / To phone, through wire, to one ear." It's not that e-composition isn't writing; but for most people, it's a different type of writing, a less contemplative and sensory mode of putting yourself into words.

There's nothing wrong with that; a speedy touch can be fun; and many written exchanges don't really need to be preserved. But some do. Some deserve a fully-embodied experience, so that we can see how the words sit on a page, touch the paper on which they were written, hear it crinkle, smell it, even lift it to our lips now and then. "I can see you undressed in your calligraphy. / I can read you over and over," says Watson. "I hold the envelope you addressed in my hand. / I hold the skin that covers you."

Personal letters require a laying-on of hands. That's part of the odd erotic thrill of a stack of antique billets-doux in a closet or attic, tied together with ribbon or string, hidden for decades from disbelieving children or grandchildren who later discover and read and (here's hoping) keep them.

11.

"A Letter always feels to me like immortality," said Emily Dickinson, letter-writer, "because it is the mind alone without corporeal friend." That's keenly phrased, and fairly unsettling: not that a letter is immortal, or imparts immortality, but that the experience of receiving and reading a letter feels like existing in some sort of solitary afterlife—a forsaken and not exactly comforting image for correspondence.

"Letters mingle souls," John Donne wrote in "To Sir Henry Wotton" several centuries earlier—a fine metaphysical notion, one quoted on a set of lovely 10-cent U.S. postage stamps in 1974, under classic paintings of people writing letters. The context for this phrase is the epistolary poem's opening: "Sir, more than kisses, letters mingle souls; / For, thus absent friends speak." Letters can connect us more profoundly than physical touch, however tender or intimate that may be; because of them, we can speak to each other when one of us is not present, "the mind alone without corporeal friend."

Voltaire is, as usual, less spiritual about it, and yet smitten with the possibilities of correspondence. "At present, without either of you leaving your apartments, you may familiarly converse through the medium of a sheet of paper," he writes in an entry in his *Philosophical Dictionary*. "The post is the grand connecting link of all transactions, of all negotiations. Those who are absent, by its means become present; it is the consolation of life."

12.

At a certain highly hormonal age, the standard parts of a letter seemed saturated with deeper meaning in my eyes. Did the object of my desire begin her note "Dear Mike," or "Dearest Michael"? Did she put "Love" or "Love always" before signing her name at the end? Even now, I sometimes mull the degrees of farewell implied in "Best," "Sincerely yours," "Yours," "xo"—does it matter, really, what words are used in that verbal equivalent of a hug or a handshake at the door?

For a number of those excitable yet lonely years, I collected stamps. I know, I know, an adolescent boy into philately is a pitiable thing, but one day my father brought some striking new stamps home from work, and I liked the way they looked and felt and smelled: before long I had albums into which I pasted them, with glassine hinges, and I was ordering inexpensive but exotic used stamps from Stanley Gibbons, and I was asking Dad to bring me plate blocks (don't ask) of the new commemorative issues. I can't recall how long this went on, but I still have the albums and envelopes in a closet somewhere, not because I want to keep them, necessarily, but because—as with that sportier young-male collection-urge, baseball cards—nobody really wants to buy them.

I enjoyed the orderliness of arranging the stamps, and also the colorful subjects of postage from foreign countries, some of which I didn't know existed. They were a way of traveling without leaving home, like the mail for which the stamps were intended. Especially for a lonesome mountain boy in western North Carolina, who would only see the Atlantic twice, briefly, before leaving the hills for college, they were little windows onto *terra incognita*.

13.

At the end of each semester, I give my poetry-writing students a charge:

"For the rest of your lives, wherever you go on this vast planet of ours, I want you to send me a tacky postcard. Not something tasteful, something you think a professor might approve of; but something strange, quirky, funny, surprising. These cards may go on the file cabinets or walls in my campus office: I hope, by the time I retire, to have covered every surface with messages and images from my far-flung poets."

Some students really rise to the challenge, and send amazing cards, a few of which have been so bawdy they had to be sealed inside an envelope. One student mailed me a coconut from Florida, with the postage stapled onto it, my address Sharpeed onto its husk, and no note: the medium truly was the message. I love having those missives surround me in my campus office, like hundreds of little poems, posted from around the globe.

Because postcards are like lyric poems. At their best, they make us feel what the writer is feeling. They are feats of concentration: every word is measured to fit the space, precisely so. They should please in phrase and image, entertaining and informing and (with any luck) moving the reader.

I don't tell my students this. I let them learn it by doing it. And I'd never mention such a thing to our many friends who have sent postcards to our home address since 1979, which I've saved in dozens of large cookie tins for future perusal and organization—one of those retirement projects that will never happen. Because I'm not a deltiologist, a scholar of *les cartes postales*: I'm an amateur, a lover of the brief, bright, personal, fun nature of this correspondence sub-genre.

14.

My wife and I always have a number of postcards magneted to our fridge. At the moment, they are: (1) The Städel Museum, from our son and daughter-in-law's trip to Germany, its message an insanely clever rebus; (2) Yellowstone National Park, an optical-illusion card from a former student and now dear friend, which—depending on the angle of viewing—is either Old Faithful or a huge bison; (3) the Durham Bulls Athletic Park, from a friend I'd sent a poem to, a seasonal image with the lined-up boys of summer honoring America during the National Anthem; and (4) *Gouffre de PADIRAC: L'Orifice*, a cave-card from France, sent by our oldest and most faithful postcard correspondent, whose densely composed messages deserve—and may yet get—their own special tin, like those I sent my wife when I was away teaching at Cornell for a semester. (A notebook entry from that time: "I haunt the mailbox like a lonely ghost.") I tried to write her a postcard every day, often from a stack bought in Cooperstown, each one featuring a different bronze plaque from the Baseball Hall of Fame gallery, including the magnificently mustachioed John Alexander "Bid" McPhee, "one of the 19th century's premier second basemen" and the last one to play without a glove. The final words of his citation are so very Scottish: "Known for his sober disposition and exemplary sportsmanship."

15.

Here's the first postcard I ever received, postmarked CRES-
CENT BEACH S.C. JUL 14 1-PM 1961 over a 3-cent Liberty
stamp, and addressed (in a mother's cursive) to "Master Mike
McFee," though the printed message is written by a six-year-old:

Dear mike,
A jelly-fish bit
Rocky. I found
sea shells.
     Love,
     Jenny

I still remember darling Jenny, whom I loved, and her well-
named brother Rocky, whom I did not: I was glad the jellyfish did
what it did. Her message seems perfect to me, exactly the right mix
of information and discovery and affection. On the picture side,
gulls still fly over empty Cherry Grove Beach, one casting its shadow on the sand, and a wavy cancellation shadows the sky over the
clouds looming along the horizon.

I may not need to say it, but I will: This silly card, mailed more
than half a century ago, chokes me up. It's an elegy for that gone
place and time and for its people, for the hand that wrote the message and for the tongue that licked the stamp. It's also an elegy for
the vanished version of me that received it. Not every saved postcard
has this effect, but enough do that I want to keep them around for a
while longer.

16.

I don't require fancy paper or envelopes to write a letter.
Sometimes, if I'm feeling classy, I'll use a sheet from the boxed ream
of vintage, cockle-finish, 100% cotton bond—with a big watermark

of the University of North Carolina seal—that a friend found in a thrift store long ago. Sometimes I'll use one of the funky postcards I've bought and saved to send to friends. Sometimes I'll invent some "stationery" with a xeroxed quote or image at the top, just for fun. But a regular sheet of paper is fine.

In a small cedar box, I have a cache of well over a hundred linen postcards—mostly from the Asheville Postcard Company, printed in the 1930s—that I'll never use or mail. Not because they're that rare or valuable, but because their colorized images of mountain scenes are so intensely lurid and weird and mesmerizing in effect. "Mount Pisgah at Sunset" looks like a Thomas Cole fever dream, and the full moon and blue clouds in "Night-Time Scene of Appalachian Hall" are melodramatically ominous, as they might have appeared to one of its mental patients.

I do try to match postcard or "stationery" and stamp to the addressee, to further personalize our exchanges by mail. When I was a design school student, I'd subvert the conventional U.S. geography of the envelopes (stamp in New England, return address in the Pacific Northwest, address in the Great Plains) with gusto, decorating them so lavishly that it was quite a challenge to find either the "From" or "To" addresses. I stopped playing this game when I discovered that the postal service did not enjoy it, and that some of my undelivered masterpieces had probably ended up in the dead-letter office.

Handwritten letters have a graphic dimension, even when it's not exaggerated, as it was by my over-clever college self. They're not merely about what happened, the contents; they're also about how the words were laid on the page by the writer's hand. That style can be as distinctive—and as welcome—as a much-missed smell.

17.

One of my professors at N.C. State's School of Design, in the early 1970s, made us buy a book called *Nomadic Furniture*, about making inexpensive furnishings—chairs, sofas, tables, beds—out of "found" materials. It gave me the idea for a desk I built back then and still write on, a lightly-water-stained, hollow-core door bought at a local hardware store for seven bucks or so, then mounted at a slight upward angle on wide homemade shelves. It's a large surface with lots of room for writing and for the stacks of poems, drafts, revisions, notebooks, dictionaries, stationery, and other arrangements of paper I need to have near me.

I wish I still had another of my design projects—clumsy and heavy and brutally ugly, but dear to my heart. The assignment was *Nomadic Furniture*-ish, i.e., take a sizable existing object and convert it to some other practical use. Somewhere in Raleigh, I found a metal air duct about four feet long, eighteen inches wide, and a foot high. For some reason, I looked at that clunky scrap and thought: if I set this up on its end, and cut it open, and add some surfaces inside, it'll make a great bookshelf.

And a mailbox. I wanted to put a mailbox—with a door that could be lowered and raised by a little metal handle, and a floor inside where letters could rest—at the top of this galvanized steel cuboid whose shelves were held in place by nuts and bolts. (I could have welded them into place in the school's shop, but I thought that exposing its structural elements would be more, uh, authentic.) I have no earthly idea why I wanted to do this, since I could never actually use the mailbox for any actual postal purposes; but I realized my plan with much effort—adding a hinged red metal flag as a final flourish—and my blunt teacher said something along the lines of "What the hell?", one of many such comments that led to my leaving the School of Design after my sophomore year, and taking up verbal rather than visual design down the road at Chapel Hill.

I used the bookshelf/mailbox through my undergrad and grad-school years—to shelve texts on its lower floors, to hide journals and letters and other private stuff in its attic—but after we got married, my wife convinced me to trash it. Which was a good idea. Even so, it did combine my emerging twin obsessions, which continue to this minute: books and the mail. I like to think of it as an object that Dickinson might have made, if she'd lived a century later, and gone to NCSU, and taken the second-year design studio: a peculiar private altar where she could arrange her volumes and store her fascicles and post her epistles to herself, since no one ever came to pick them up: "This is my letter to the World / That never wrote to Me."

18.

Back in my mid-twenties, I wrote and somehow managed to publish a poem called "The Mailman." It is, to put it kindly, not very good, though it wrestles gamely with a number of things later addressed in more successful work.

It's nice to be pleasantly surprised by an old weak poem, if only for a phrase or line, and this passage caught my eye: "he should be heard but not seen, / like St. Nick in an Old-Glory-colored sleigh / whistling up the block with a sackful of treats." There's way too much going on there—"like St. Nick with a sackful of treats" might be sufficient—but I'm grateful for the postman-as-Santa image. On a good mail day, that captures my almost childlike feeling of anticipation quite nicely.

"As long as there are postmen," said the philosophical William James, "life will have zest."

19.

A mail slot in a house's front door always seemed so sophisticated, so big-city, like a domestic version of the brass-and-glass mail chutes in old high-rises. What a luxury, to have the mailman walk directly to your entry six days a week, and lift the slot's protective outer flap, and push the day's offerings inside, spilling onto the hall floor!

I loved being at my grandmother's in Asheville when the mail came. I'd run to the front door and try to catch the letters as they fell from above, manna from postal heaven.

20.

My dad worked at the post office for "34 years and 9 months," as his retirement papers say, "of creditable service." He was a window clerk briefly, early on, but mostly he was one of those behind-the-scenes guys in the back who distribute and expedite the mail. Apparently, he didn't mind such anonymity, or working the graveyard shift for much of his career, since it paid a slightly higher wage for handling mail in the middle of the night while the mailers and mailees were at home asleep. He left the house about the time we all went to bed, a bit after 11 P.M.; he returned around 9 A.M., shortly after my sister and I went to school, and slept all day while we were away.

Christmases could be peculiar. Back when everybody used the U.S. Mail, and when most everybody sent Christmas cards, the flood of holiday mail was so overwhelming that Dad would sometimes have to work back-to-back eight-hour shifts, which paid well but took a physical toll. A few times, on Christmas morning, he didn't get home till after we impatient kids had already started opening presents. That surely took an emotional toll.

For years, my father had to memorize Asheville's streets and addresses in a particular way, so he'd know how to sort the mail and which carrier to give it to, without having to consult a coding guide. There were many mimeographed pages of such information, address ranges and delivery routes, and he'd ask me to quiz him on the names and numbers, in random order, so he'd be able to make the quickest possible decisions. I'd say something like "Patton Avenue, 1 to 500," and he'd answer quickly with an alphabetical code, like "A." "Biltmore Road" (not "Avenue" or "Street," a tricky distinction: there were many local subtleties of nomenclature and spelling): "B."

"Merrimon Avenue, 1000 to 2000": "C." "Arlington Street." He'd smile at that before answering, since he grew up at 76 Arlington, and could imagine his mother's narrow old house at the bottom of the hill, and the carrier making two steps across the porch, and the ghosts of his mother or aunt retrieving the mail he could sort in his sleep.

21.

I have a relic from Dad's handling and distributing and dispatching career, something he used while processing the mail in the wee hours. Shortly after he died, I wrote a poem about it, triggered by a sighting at my bank:

Rubber Finger Tip

Little latex thimble,
how snugly you top
the teller's pinkie,
an amber mini-condom
flipping stacked bills,
protecting her touch
from dry filthy cash:
the rubber thumb cap
my clerk-father wore,
its nubs besmutted
by millions of letters,
still smells like sweat
despite the seven holes
venting its brittle back.

That dry, brown rubber finger tip looked like the top of an amputated thumb, cut from a glove.

22

I'll admit: It's not much fun to visit most post offices today. USPS buildings and lobbies are typically uninspiring, the lines are often long and slow, and the clerks are not particularly engaged or friendly.

Once upon a time not so long ago, the post office was central to its municipality, and its appearance—like a bank or a county courthouse—reflected that importance. I remember Mom taking me into the downtown P.O. in Asheville as a kid, where Dad worked, and being awed at the look and sound and smell of the place, all that brass and marble, and all those rented mailboxes in the walls like numbered safes whose combinations only the owners knew, though I could spy their contents through little windows in their metal doors.

Usually, I buy stamps and mail packages at an uncrowded USPS Contract Postal Unit in the basement of UNC's student stores, a two-minute stroll from the English building. But I still make excuses to walk to the downtown post office in Chapel Hill, a couple of quads north and across Franklin Street from campus. Though smaller than its bigger-city cousins, it still has the feel of a vintage P.O., and with a bonus on the wall overhead: an autumnal New Deal mural completed in 1941, showing the "Laying of the Cornerstone of Old East," the oldest public-university dormitory in the country, which I've just walked past. What pleases me about this overhead painting is not its quality—perfectly fine, though hardly great—but its very existence, which is pretty much how I feel about the U.S. Mail itself. At a challenging time in our nation's history, these murals were commissioned to bring art to public buildings and make it accessible to all people, a mighty complicated undertaking. Making the paintings and sculptures and terra cotta or plaster reliefs local in their focus was crucial: that's precisely why they work, because they're firmly rooted in the community's culture.

And that's the beauty of at least the idea of the postal service: prompt delivery of the mail to all people, in the city or the countryside, so that what you send from your home or business can be carried to any other individual address in a couple of days, by a person who knows closely the streets and roads of that particular place. From the appointment of Benjamin Franklin as first postmaster general in 1775, to the creation of City Free Delivery in 1863, to the introduction of Rural Free Delivery in 1896, through the steady expansion and automation of the post office in the twentieth century, to the uncertain present day, nothing could be more reassuringly American than the mission of universal postal service at affordable rates. The mail makes our impossibly diverse nation a community: once a day, Monday through Saturday, we can correspond with, and to, each other.

23.

Mail carriers have a letter-perfect unofficial motto: "Neither snow nor rain nor heat nor gloom of night stays these couriers from the swift completion of their appointed rounds." It's ancient in origin, an adaptation/translation from Herodotus, who in his *Histories* was describing the Persian system of mounted postal carriers, circa 500 B.C.E.: "It is said that as many days as there are in the whole journey, so many are the men and horses that stand along the road, each horse and man at the interval of a day's journey; and these are stayed neither by snow nor rain nor heat nor darkness from accomplishing their appointed course with all speed."

Though the original is interesting—especially for the presence of horses, which may be how "post" got attached to mail delivery—I think I prefer the Americanized version. It has more rhetorical momentum, and "gloom of night" is a nice tonal intensifying of "darkness," those sad black hours when no letters are delivered, though they're on their way. And I like landing on those circular "rounds," a ripe noun with overtones of music and sport and drink. A round of applause for these couriers! Cheers!

24.

There really is something about a letter carrier in uniform: the crisp shirt with the USPS logo, the pants or shorts with the natty tuxedo stripes down the side, the pith-like helmet sometimes worn against the sun. Men and women alike may hate it, but it makes me happy that they dress up to deliver our mail, presenting themselves in a casually decorous way. Maybe I should return the favor now and then: "I can wait at the mailbox with my hair combed, / In my best suit," as Robert Watson writes. I think our mailwoman would be amused.

When I was a kid, the mail was often delivered by carriers in Jeeps, which added to the military air. They were solid blue below, unlike the mostly white current mail vehicles, but they had the same steering wheel and sliding door on the passenger side, in the British manner, and the same encircling bold red stripe, as if a deconstructed Old Glory paraded up and down our streets every week of the year.

25.

Back in the late 1970s, as poetry editor for *Carolina Quarterly*, I had to leave some proofs in Reynolds Price's mailbox, out in Durham County. That unofficial mail delivery changed my postal life, because he had the biggest residential box I'd ever seen, capacious enough for piles of letters and magazines and books, perfect for a writer and reader obsessed with the mail.

Eventually, I had my own, a 23 ½ x 11 ½ x 13 ½ inch giant. U.S. MAIL, it said on the door, APPROVED BY THE POST-MASTER GENERAL. My wife and I sank a wooden post in concrete out by the road, affixed the corrugated gray box to the solid crossing arm, and I've enjoyed it roughly 300 times a year for more than half my life.

I once helped my father put up a regular-sized mailbox for our family in Royal Pines. It was across the street from our house, on the odd side, so I helpfully painted it the same green color as our house, then lettered our surname on it in black enamel, to make certain our box was not confused with our redneck neighbor's, drunkenly tilted a few feet away. At some point, we indulged in a brushed-metal address sign, a thick plaque firmly bolted to the top of the box (no mere stick-on letters for us!):

W. H. McFEE
160 LOCUST COURT

it said, a handsome announcement of patriarch and place on both sides, so you'd know us coming and going.

There's nothing like that on my own mailbox now, in these more identity-protective days. But I unbolted Dad's sign from the box after my parents died and the house was sold, bringing it back here to my Durham home, where it crowns a bookcase. I've kept it to remind me of him now and then, and of a time when the U.S. Mail was more central to life in the U.S. of A., even in a lower-middle-class suburb of Asheville, in the once-remote mountains of North Carolina. It's not exactly a grave marker, and yet it is.

26.

I write a lot of e-mails. Some of them are "virtual post-it notes," as one friend characterizes them, but others are much more like the paper letters I've written for so long. I respond with care to thoughtfully-written incoming e-missives, proofing and improving my message before hitting "Send." Though they may be delivered almost instantly and in an impermanent format, words should still take a while to write well.

Have I preserved these more deliberate e-mails, as I would similar letters? Yes, going back to January 3, 2000: I currently have nearly 9,000 or so messages in my "Personal Mail Worth Saving" file in Gmail, averaging more than one a day over seventeen-plus years. What do I plan to do with all those electronic epistles? I can't imagine printing them out—so many reams, so much ink. And yet, I'm glad that verbal record exists: it's as close as I'll ever come to diary, or autobiography, and I like it better than either of those genres, since correspondence always involves another person, a co-respondent, and not merely my tiresome self.

27.

I've had some meaningful clusters of correspondence over the years, sustained exchanges with distant friends, many of them writers—Robert Morgan, Jonathan Williams, Shirley Anders, Jack Butler, and Alvaro Cardona-Hine in New Mexico, who, even as he neared ninety, wrote letters that were eloquent and audacious and deeply beautiful. My heart lifted up when I beheld his return address on an envelope in my mailbox. These long-distance conversations-on-paper (with pauses built into our dialogues by distance and time: one must wait for an unrushed response from the other party) are like chapters in a collaborative work-in-progress, an epistolary non-fiction novel that will never be finished though it will certainly end.

My most faithful correspondent has been Aunt Mickey, my late mother's youngest sister, and a steady inspiration to me since I was a boy. She was the first adult I saw writing poetry, and taking it seriously; she read writers and thinkers like Carl Jung; she was a charming visual artist, and a devoted parent/grandparent/great-grandparent—she was a muse, to me and to many others. Until her mid-eighties, if I wrote Mickey, she always wrote back within a few days from her mountain home, passionate smart enthusiastic letters penned in her distinctive hand, the lines so steady and straight that it looked like she must have used a ruler under them, though she said she didn't. Mickey exemplified correspondence at its best, a word whose root means "to promise": she kept the fundamental promise of letter-writing, which is *If you write me, I'll write you,* never letting a silence fall as we talked through the mails, across the miles, over the years.

28.

Maybe I got the letter-writing gene from the maternal side of the family. My late mother, like her little sister, was also an active correspondent. She'd sit down with a cup of coffee and a cigarette, and a cheap unlined notepad and a ballpoint pen, and, with her arthritic hand, write me (or later, after marriage, us) the latest news from 160 Locust Court. Her letters were remarkably like her: droll, chatty, alert, wryly fatalistic, deeply affectionate. Once I left home for college, I don't think a week went by that at least one Letter from Lucy didn't arrive, whether or not I found the time to write her back.

I still have one dated "Feb. 19th," and addressed to my wife and nearly-three-year-old son and me in Ithaca, New York, where I was poet-in-residence at Cornell for 1986–1987. "I know that weather is no big deal for you," she starts, "but today we have had rain, sleet, and snow and the weather man says 2 inches of ice covered the county and another storm is forming which will probably be snow. For several years now we haven't had enough snow to measure but we seem to be making up for that." After reporting on the "bug" they've all endured down in North Carolina, and after a sweet paragraph addressed to our son, including a drawing of a "snow man named Philip," she concludes: "I really have no news since I'm in hibernation but have thought of you all day and wanted you to know / we love you, / Mom, Dad & Steph."

She posted that letter—so typical in its tone, in its "have thought of you all day and wanted you to know" sentiment—on

Friday, February 20, 1987. She suffered a cerebral hemorrhage a few days later; I caught the first flight I could, but she died early on Tuesday the 24th, before I arrived. Given the lag time in delivery, I didn't read my mother's last letter until I returned to Ithaca, after her funeral down in Asheville.

29.

"An odd thought strikes me," said Samuel Johnson, in December of 1784: "We shall receive no letters in the grave." Or compose them either: what a basic human pleasure, not only to receive letters, but to sit down and slow down and write down heartfelt, thoughtful words on paper, addressed to someone you call "Dear," hoping for something in return.

How many letters have I written or received, in my six decades of life? Many, many, many tens of thousands. A man of letters, literally, I've tried to save the ones that meant the most to me, both outgoing and incoming: those teetering stacks of handwritten or typed (with carbons) or printed-out correspondence are waiting in a huge trunk under my desk, and I'm still adding to the archives.

Why? Neither my wife nor son will be interested in all that old mail, once I'm gone. I doubt I'll ever go back and read those *Selected Letters* myself, though I'd like to, to get a picture of what my previous selves were like, to hear those younger versions of my voice, and to be reminded of what life was like through the days and months and years: that's much of the interest of anybody's letters, those unexpected details helping us feel the texture of time past.

Why do I save them? One reason, really: Because, for me, letters are writing. No less than a poem, or this essay, a personal letter is a literary composition. It requires a certain level of attention and intensity and focus—but not too much, which is the glory of correspondence: in the writing and in the reading, it feels looser somehow, less self-conscious, and often sounds more like the writer's everyday, playful, worried, yearning, true self. Isn't that the charm of

Keats's letters? Though very different from his odes, they are still delightful and casually brilliant writing, words that intrigue and please several centuries later.

"I do not care if I am writing a poem or a letter," says Mary Ruefle: "it is just making marks on a sheet of paper that delights and envelops me. What I am trying to tell you is this: every time you write an unengaged letter, you are wasting another opportunity to be a writer."

30.

I know, I know, I know. I know that the volume and quality of my mail—sent and received—are declining, and I assume everybody else's are, too. I know that younger generations communicate electronically and could care less about the mail as it has traditionally existed, as I have elegized it: for them, loving the mail is like loving a daily print newspaper or a manual typewriter—what's the point, these days? I know that the conventional USPS seems to be doomed by internal and external factors, that it's threatening to cut Saturday delivery to save expenses, that it's hardly as noble as I've imagined it: how disheartening to read, in the *New York Times* of July 4, 2013, about the "Mail Isolation Control and Tracking program, in which Postal Service computers photograph the exterior of every piece of paper mail that is processed in the United States" making that information available to law enforcement officials looking for criminal activity.

And yet, there's still something about the mail that I can't shake, and never will. Michael Chitwood and I could swap comments about each other's poems in person (we both teach at UNC), or by e-mail; but we've done it through the mail for a quarter-century or so, sending paper copies of new work to each other so that we can read and mark and inwardly digest them, then seal those collaborative words into an envelope and send them back. The reliable rhythm of that exchange, the expectation and satisfaction of it, the thought of all those lines and stanzas shuttling between his house and mine, all these years—it's kept me going during some mighty lean times, poetically and otherwise. *I need to get something in the mail to Mike*, I'll think, and head to the desk again.

This would not have been possible without the mail, whose blue thread helps keep us stitched together.

31.

In one dream of heaven, every time I visit my celestial mailbox it's full, no matter how much I remove or leave there. And every piece inside is pure gospel, a personal letter or card, a grateful acceptance from a first-rate magazine, a new book by a friend or former student or even by myself, one I'd forgotten was coming out: everything I behold uplifts my postal soul. It's like coming home after a long journey, to a month's worth of the mail, patiently held at the P.O. then delivered as requested, all those words waiting for me to take them in hand, and read them without rushing, and start thinking about what I want to write in response, the correspondence continuing without end.

3.

CLOTH

H*ardback* may be the better word for it, a more accurate complement to *paperback*, a good, solid compound word that says what it is and shows what it means.

But I prefer the use of *cloth* for non-paper editions of a book. That monosyllable has a more elegant air: one dresses in cloth, and a cloth version of a volume is its most dressed-up self, formal evening wear instead of casual daytime duds.

It sounds better, too. *Cloth* involves the tongue and teeth in a more sensual way. And it has holy associations, as in "a man of the cloth," someone—like an author—with a true vocation and not just a job.

Cloth editions are more expensive to produce, obviously. That may be why I've only had one cloth edition of any of my eleven books of poems (and that was library binding, a cheaper process): why spend more money to make a book that's already going to lose money? This non-cloth approach to publishing has trickled down to prose as well, with New York houses and major university presses issuing literary fiction and non-fiction in "paperback original" formats.

Libraries once wanted cloth books for their shelves—they held up better through the years—but those flush pre-digital days appear to be long gone. And once upon a time, picky readers wanted cloth editions, with dustjackets, for their private collections: they looked great, they endured, they were more valuable. But the numbers of those collectors have also dwindled, perhaps unhappily ever after.

Does any of this really matter? A book is a book, no matter how it's bound: its gathering of pages can still be bought or checked out and read. And a paperback volume still has more actual volume than an e-book. Is the distinction, finally, one of tone? Compared with a hardback, even the nicest paperback can feel a bit flimsy or ephemeral. A cloth edition, its boards bound neatly in fabric, seems more solid in the hand, more protective of the book's precious contents, and more permanent in the mind of its writer and reader.

INSCRIPTIONS

What luck!—to write a book, to have a publisher print and distribute it, and then to have someone present it to you for a signature or personalized inscription. What an honor, to have friends or strangers spend their money on your work, and to want your living name written on it, as if it were a painting to be hung on a wall.

True, very true. And yet it's also true that inscriptions can be hard to do well: on the spot, you must think up something original and appropriate to write on the half-title or title page of this book you took so long to make, something that this person and others may read with pleasure and appreciation, immediately and in future years. It's a literary version of signing somebody's yearbook, except that yours is the only inscription in it, and since you're a writer it should be instantly clever, insightful, touching.

Some writers don't worry about this. They simply write the same thing every time, for every person: one poet has signed many books to me (and others?) exactly the same way, "With admiration and affection." And some writers won't inscribe at all: they simply sign their names, which is probably better for collectors but is disappointing if you'd hoped for a more personal touch. That book now feels like a signed contract between author and reader—not an inaccurate image, but it's hard to have warm feelings about a legal document.

Me, I inscribe, and I try to make each one different, thoughtful, sincere. This means I sometimes, if not often, fail. But I give it a shot, always asking people how to spell their names: once, at a reading where I was selling my own stock, I inscribed a book to a woman and handed it to her, and she handed it right back, saying,

"I want one where you spell my name right." That became a reading copy, and a useful lesson.

In local used bookshops, I've found a few volumes that I inscribed. At first, it hurt me to see them there: how could she sell this volume with its beautiful personal note, how could he bear to let this, with its heartfelt inscription, go? But now it mostly makes me sad: people sell their books for all kinds of reasons, including the need for money or shelf space, and occasionally signed copies show up as part of an estate, a former library scattered, another reader gone. And if I don't remember the person I signed the book to— any more than that person remembered me with enough fondness to keep it—I simply leave the inscribed volume on the shelves: maybe someone with the same first name will buy or receive it one day.

Years ago, I asked a fellow poet and collector why he had gathered so many inscribed volumes. "A signed book completes the circle begun in manuscript," he said, and I liked that image a lot: what began with the author's hand concludes with it, and brings you as close to the moment of composition as it's possible to get. I liked his idea so much that I began asking my friends and other writers to sign volumes of theirs that I'd bought, read, loved, held on to: those inscriptions surround me now throughout my house, hospitable reminders of where books come from, other human beings who also put words on paper, hoping to please a reader who might someday walk toward them, book extended, and say, "Would you sign this, please?"

TO'S AND FOR'S

How important are dedications at the beginning of a book or poem? How essential is "To A" or "For B" to the work, to the reader's understanding or appreciating it?

For books, that's partly a structural question. A "dedication page" is part of the traditional front matter of a volume, often between the copyright page and the table of contents. The twelfth edition of the *Chicago Manual of Style* is quite stern about it: "Extravagant dedications are things of the past. A dedication intended to be humorous will very likely lose its humor with time and so is inappropriate in a serious book destined to take a permanent place in the literature." Sir, yes sir!

For most books, a dedication is more custom than clue. Writers have dedicated books to others they admire for a long time: it's an affectionate gesture, not a crucial textual key. Most of us make symbolic gifts of our work <u>To</u> long-suffering spouses and children, or <u>For</u> helpful friends, and there are plenty of those folks to keep us in dedicatees for our entire career. Sometimes there are surprises at the front of a volume—A. R. Ammons' dedication of *The Snow Poems* was "For my country"—but writers typically present their books to other humans.

Dedicating individual poems is a trickier matter—more personal, more intimate really, and easier to mishandle. If, between title and text, there's an epigraphic line "To Y" or "For Z," it implies that this person is somehow an inspiration or direct influence on this particular poem. Which is to say, it's an inside reference, something private made public; and how absolutely necessary is that? This practice or habit can feel like namedropping, especially if there are numerous poems dedicated to well-known contemporary writers: it's virtue by association, and rather off-putting, even if the dedications are segregated en masse elsewhere in the book. Can't the poor poems stand on their own?

And which is better when dedicating, "To" or "For"? "To" sounds more poetic and odic, besides being the first word in the infinitive verb form. But "For" has its quadratic, points-of-the-compass, corners-of-the-page charm. I seem to favor the latter: my first three books were "To's," and two of them to the memory of parents; but since 1994, I've gone for "For's," for some reason— fellow writers and readers and supporters, son and wife and niece, and, in an expansive flourish, "For my students, teachers, colleagues, and many friends at UNC-Chapel Hill over the past quarter-century." I'm glad I did that. It demonstrates what dedications are about: not the writer who put the words on the page, but a larger community that was also part of the work's composition, without which it might never have come into being, in this particular form. Their names up front may not explain anything, but they can mean everything.

RECTO AND VERSO

I love these terms for the right- and left-hand pages in a book. They sound like a vaudeville comedy team—*Ladies and gentlemen, Recto and Verso!*—and in a way they are, a trick act where one is the flip side of the other and then becomes the other when turned.

Recto. How fitting, that the first actual page of a book is literally *on the right side.* And the book's most visibly "important" pages—half-title, title, beginning of text and chapters—are indeed on the front side of the leaf, foursquare and brimming with rectitude.

Verso. What could be better, in a book of verse, than to have a verso page, lines being broken and turned on *the page being turned?* And though the front side of leaves may get the most attention, isn't it the reverse side—the back side, the underside, the down side—that's often most interesting to writers? That's where the story may be stirring, over on that shady plot.

I don't know why these terms developed as *recto* and *verso*, instead of *dexter* and *sinister*, Latin for "right" and "left." But they sound better this way, and the metaphorical implications may be richer.

The verso page always has the last word: it's the final rectangle of textual matter before the endpapers start. Though it may be blank, it's a conclusion, a benediction, an empty narthex echoing with the recessional, saying, "Wait. Be quiet. Stand still in this doorway, before leaving the printed sanctuary behind."

LOOK AND SOUND

Doris Betts would say to her fiction-writing students: "If a writer's kid brother were reading this story aloud in a tone of ridicule, could the story survive?"

That's a funny and wise test, and sometimes it comes to mind when I'm reading work printed in a bad typeface or on poor paper: does it have the objective verbal durability to survive this visual insult?

I started college as a design student, many decades ago, but I'm not a font snob. Though I prefer the elegance of serif letters, and print my own work in Garamond or Times New Roman, I can read a page of sans-serif text without distress. Some typefaces seem more handsome to me, but as long as your personal preference isn't some kind of overwrought script, I'm not going to complain.

Even so, some looks are better than others. The 1976 edition of Auden's *Collected Poems* was memorably bad: the poetry was set in a clunky typewriter-esque typeface, the paper seemed cheap, and the pages of my copy kept falling out of the spine—what was Random House thinking? Not that all poetry must be printed by letterpress, on handcrafted sheets, in limited editions; but this design did a great injustice to great work.

I wish most students didn't encounter poetry only in fat anthologies like *The Norton Anthology of Poetry*. It's printed on opaque Bible paper (understandable, given its girth) and so the pages are flimsy, the ghost of the poem on the verso page haunting the one being read, which imparts a certain insubstantiality to the many poems in this Greatest Hits. I loan each of my poetry-writing students an individual volume by a contemporary poet during the semester, to confirm that they know what a well-designed and well-printed book of poems looks and feels like, to the eye and hand.

Every so often, I change the font or size of my work, to shake the page up and help me encounter the words in a new way; but I always come back to the familiar settings. By now, it's like seeing my voice or my accent—a particular timbre or color or pitch—captured on paper. I'm sure other writers do the same thing, and a book's designer as well: Which font, which paper, which layout will express the true nature of this writing? Which look best suits the sound?

COPY

For catalogue and publicity purposes, my publisher asked me to write a three-sentence description of my latest book of poems. While I appreciate the opportunity to summarize what I've done, rather than having somebody else do it, I must admit: I wish somebody else *would* do it. Because—having spent many years inside the poetry, working to make every syllable right—it's mighty difficult to step back from it and see clearly what I've been trying to do, then convert eighty-four pages of implicitness into three blasts of snappy and catchy copy.

But I did it. I wrestled that reticent book to the ground, and won. But something kept bothering me, and finally I realized: the copy sounded familiar. So I looked back at the three-sentence descriptions of my previous books with the same publisher, and found I'd written basically the same thing, each time. Not that the books were the same, but the process of crafting promotional prose was apparently a formulaic one for me, and resulted in weirdly similar summaries. I knew that some poets wrote the same poem over and over again, but this was ridiculous.

Ridiculous, yes, but not—to my eye and ear—unusual. If you read enough jacket or catalogue copy, it all starts to sound alike: there are details specific to each book, but in general a soft-focus lens, an upbeat tone, and some familiar hyperbolic phrases are the rule. Certain terms are used and reused, to pitch this particular kind of product.

I've always thought that the best possible copy for a book of poetry would be simply to print one of the strongest or most representative poems in the book on the back cover. That way, potential readers won't have to go digging for that gem before purchasing: it's there, they can read it and decide, no prose is needed to convince them they're holding a winner. (That might also be the most helpful review for a book of poetry: simply print a few of the best—and worst—poems in the volume, then get out of the way.) But such an approach would be preaching to the poetic choir. If poetry is ever to reach the world of non-poets, it must be advertised in prose, however unoriginal that copy seems.

BLURBS

I admit: I have committed blurbs. Like most writers who have been at it for a while, I sometimes agree to write a few sentences of praise for a forthcoming book, in the hopes that my words might help persuade a potential reader not to put the book back on the shelf, to keep it and buy it and take it home and read it and possibly feel as I did after I read it: happy.

I once had to solicit blurbs for a new book of poems, though my publisher—a fine university press, and therefore terribly overworked and understaffed, which must be why I was doing the soliciting—hadn't used the blurbs I procured for my previous collection. I hate approaching friends for blurbs: it's a huge favor to ask, like requesting yet another letter of recommendation except that they have to read an entire manuscript and think hard about it and then condense their enthusiasms to a few crisp sentences of endorsement. No rush, no pressure, but we need your pithiness by next Friday!

Blurbs are hard to do, or at least, to do well, in an original and insightful manner. Bad ones sound like the excerpted and clichéd praise on theater marquees. Good ones are themselves little works of art, their well-chosen words opening a window onto the words inside the book. I was surprised and pleased to see—among the "Literary Statements and Reviews" in the Library of America's *Elizabeth Bishop: Prose, Poems, and Letters*—five blurbs that Bishop did for books of poems, each one getting at the essence of that book in her own most distinctive voice.

"Blurb" is a fairly ugly word, a sonic hybrid of "blurt" and "disturb"—or, if you're feeling ironic, maybe "bluff" and "superb"? It was invented by American humorist Gelett Burgess (author of the "I never saw a purple cow" quatrain), who produced a fake dustjacket with a young woman on it, Miss Belinda Blurb, "in the act of blurbing." Which is to say, it originated as a joke, though in the century since it has become much more earnest in tone. Perhaps blurbs should recover some of their original playfulness, since, as Gurney Norman observed, every blurber is basically saying, "This is a perfectly acceptable book by a friend of mine."

Eventually, I got an eloquent, thoughtful blurb from an old friend of mine, a terrific critic and poet I hadn't imposed on before, and I sent it on to the press, not knowing if they would use it on the cover at all. That would have been fine with me: the newborn book would arrive in the world unencumbered by endorsements, so that the only words selling it to the prospective reader would be my own, the ones that took so many years to write.

NEW BOOK

January 19, 2012: a cold gray Thursday, early in the spring term. My wife phones me on campus, a rare pleasure. "Your book came!" she says—my new collection of poetry: I'd expected it to arrive soon. "Great!" I say, "How does it look?" "I don't know," she says, in a hurry, "I just got home and the dog needs to go pee."

Ah, the glamorous life of the poet.

It's not a life I ever thought I'd actually be living. But I am, and I have been, and (muses willing) I will continue to be. This is my fourteenth published book and eighth full-length collection of poems, numbers beyond imagining back in 1975 when I was a clueless undergraduate on this same campus, starting my first poetry-writing class.

I'll start giving readings from the book—a four-town local tour, at good independent stores—next month and end it in April. Some copies will be sold and signed, e.g., "To X, these verbal oases: hope they give pleasure!" And I'll submit it for a few prizes, as usual. But mostly, feedback from the literary world will be minimal; as Don Marquis said, "Publishing a volume of verse and waiting for the response is like dropping a rose petal down the Grand Canyon and waiting for the echo." Or as Charles Wright put it, "Publishing a book of poetry is like lighting a firecracker in the middle of the Atlantic Ocean."

But hasn't that almost always been true? Aren't the best responses personal, when a friend or stranger surprises you by saying how much she enjoyed the book or one of its poems? (Flash forward: half a year later, my neighbor writes: "I just read several of your new poems to my friend at the nursing home, including the last one in the book. As I sobbed through the final two lines, she patted me and said, 'Don't try to stop it, just let it flow.' We also laughed out loud at a couple." Maybe I'm a sap, but I doubt the poetry Pulitzer could make me happier.)

Today is a very rare pleasure: I have a new book. It exists in the world, a physical fact and artifact, another installment in whatever lifelong writing project it is that I'm undertaking. For now, I'm in the honeymoon—or, more accurately, new parent—stage: grinning, giddy, feeling absurdly lucky.

4.

MY *NEW YORKER*

1.

January 19, 1987. (A wintry Monday; *The New Yorker* continues to be published on the first working day of the week in 2013, though it usually arrives shortly before its pub date.)

Price: $1.50. (Price in 2013: $6.99—almost a 500-percent increase in twenty-six years. And now this amount appears to the left rather than the right of "*The*" in the apparently unchanged *New Yorker* name on the cover, that fancy display typeface like letterhead on stationery.)

Cover: a nighttime-blue ice-skating scene by Arthur Getz, sketchy silhouettes on a rural pond, bonfire blazing on the shore, cabin windows glowing in the background. (These days, covers are given names on the full-page list of contents, which is no longer identified as the Table of Contents.)

Table of Contents (a small insert on page two back then, a list tucked into the beginning of Goings On about Town): The Talk of the Town; non-fiction pieces by Polly Frost, E. J. Kahn, Jr., and Wallace White; reviews by Brendan Gill and John Updike; drawings by William Steig, Charles Saxon, Gahan Wilson, Ed Arno, Edward Koren, and a dozen others; fiction by Francine Prose; a profile by Calvin Tomkins; a long "Letter from New Delhi" by Ved Mehta; and poems by L. S. Asekoff, Derek Walcott, and—on page 69, following that 17-page report from India, at the very bottom of the page—Michael McFee. Me. A poet, for all the world to see, with a poem in the magazine where every poet wanted to appear, *The New Yorker*. Or—as I thought of it then and think of it to this day, holding the magazine (its pages slightly wider, its type a bit more compact than now) in the hands that had written and rewritten then typed and retyped those words and lines and stanzas, before folding them into an envelope and mailing them to Manhattan for consideration—my *New Yorker*.

2.

I was introduced to *The New Yorker* in the mid-1970s, by a college poetry professor. In those pre-photocopy days, he would bring the latest issue to class and read us its poems, then pass it around so we Chapel Hill undergraduates could appreciate its text in print and in sophisticated big-city context. He also had stacks of copies in his bookish house near campus, archives of wonderful writing and cartoons close to hand in every room.

I was smitten. And though I was comically poor—I had a part-time job in the library, and owned one pair of over-patched jeans, a couple of t-shirts and flannel shirts, and a pair of Clarks desert boots—I took out a student subscription, so that my small room could be brightened by *New Yorkers* slowly climbing toward the ceiling, layer by papery layer. And I've been a subscriber ever since.

3.

Once I started taking writing seriously, I began submitting to *The New Yorker*, like every other ambitious scribbler. My ancient index-card file tells me that I first submitted on August 13, 1979, and received this reply: "No manuscripts read from March 28th to September 4th." And thus did the naïve young writer learn a useful lesson: many magazines don't consider submissions during the summer.

So I tried again on October 19th, with the same three poems I'd sent back in August, and a few more thrown in. No luck: rejected. Ditto for the next three submissions, in subsequent years.

I was submitting poems elsewhere, of course, and getting rejected regularly. But I was also starting to get accepted and published, and making my way toward a first book of poetry, which was published late in 1983. How proud I was! And yet, I couldn't stop thinking about *The New Yorker*: that's where I really, really, really wanted to be.

4.

I'd been a waiter—sorry: working scholar—at Bread Loaf in the summer of 1980. While not particularly inspiring or instructive to me as a writer, or quite the career breakthrough I'd imagined, the conference was two weeks of beery fun, and I met some fellow poets who became friends. One was Henri Cole, who—as executive director of the Academy of American Poets—invited me to New York to take part in a New Voices reading at the Donnell Library on Thursday, February 9, 1984.

J. D. "Sandy" McClatchy introduced us, and I think was the second reader. I know I followed Nicholas Christopher, whose dark outfit and minimalist reading style set up my Southern affability pretty well. And I know I admired Katha Pollitt and her poems. But I don't remember much about the reading itself.

I'll never forget the aftermath, though. Some of the smallish crowd had come down front to greet the poets, to chat and mingle for a while. My back to the auditorium stage, I was talking with Henri when suddenly people began to step aside, to make way so that someone could pass through: a balding man, headed in my direction, of average size and looks, wearing a pair of largish wire-rim glasses and a heavy, dark raincoat that was buttoned or held shut.

I didn't know what to expect—after all, I was a hick in New York in the mid-1980s. Was he going to flash me? Shoot me? Arrest me?

"Mr. McFee," he said, extending his hand, "I enjoyed your poems. I'm Howard Moss, poetry editor of *The New Yorker*."

5.

I managed not to faint, or to squeal with joy or terror, or to shriek, "OH, MY GOD!"—though all of those things very nearly happened. We had a pleasant, brief conversation during which he invited me to send some poems to him at the magazine, "when you have some available." *When I have some available?* It was all I could do not to stuff the poems I'd just read into his coat pockets, saying, "Please! Sir! Take anything you like! I have lots more!"

I restrained myself for a few weeks, once back home in North Carolina, but finally sent him some available poems on February 28th. Within a few weeks, Mr. Moss returned them with a signed note, saying, "Thank you for letting us see them, and we look forward to others." He and I went back and forth several more times over the next year or two, until I sent him a fresh batch on March 10, 1986, my son's second birthday—surely that would bring good luck, right? (I probably made Philip kiss the envelope, before I posted it with my usual charge: "Bring back an acceptance!")

And then it came, the letter of my dreams:

April 18, 1986

Dear Mr. McFee,

I'm delighted to say we're taking SNOW GOAT, and I hope to have an author's proof and a check to send along soon.

I hope this is the first of many poems of yours to appear in *The New Yorker* and thanks for sending it to us. We look forward to others.

Best wishes,

Howard Moss.

Here's the irony of that glorious news: the poem he accepted, "Snow Goat," was the last one I put in the envelope. I thought the other three somewhat longer poems were much stronger, but I figured it couldn't hurt to toss a sonnet into the poetic ring, given Mr. Moss's fondness for form. Even so, I was surprised that he took what I'd thought of as an experiment in technique and narrative, an exercise in rhyme and meter, an aside.

But the more I considered it, and especially once it appeared in the magazine, I thought: You know, this really is one of the best poems I've ever written.

And I kept going back to Howard Moss's sublime words: "I hope this is the first of many poems of yours to appear in *The New Yorker*." That was better than the acceptance itself, the promise of a future in the pages of the greatest general-circulation literary magazine ever, the possibility that I could become a regular contributor, a lifetime member of The Club.

I also took his "We look forward to others" too seriously too soon, sending him a new group of poems on April 25th. He returned them with a kind note saying, "We look forward to more this fall." I figured I should wait till after my poem was published to submit again, and did.

6.

"Only religious loyalties ever united the villages and the cities, the poor and the rich—the two Indias," concluded Ved Mehta. "But the cohesive force that religion once provided is now dissolving with the resurgence of fundamentalism in the dominant religions, and the attendant reactionism, fascism, and intolerance." Prophetic as those words have proven, at the time they exasperated me, because they were delaying the reader's pleasure in getting to my poem—if, indeed, any reader persisted through all that text and all those ads to read:

Snow Goat

Stirred by the snow's rare erasure, my sister
hikes across backyards quiet as a bedroom
into the ruin-rich woods where Jack kissed her,
then disappeared beyond the briers and gloom.

Who cares? she says, skiing shallow ravines
behind the vacant sausage plant. *What a bore.*
I hope he gets killed in Korea with the Marines
or Army. Nothing could surprise me anymore.

Then the snow at her elbow says *bah* and there
he is, shocking as God, white, his slitted eye
golden with curiosity. He tongues the bare
salt lick of her hand, and she starts to cry,
fearing his cloven hooves and her desire
sharp as those horns whetted on the wire.

In those pre-internet days, response to "Snow Goat"—to my
New Yorker—was much slower. But it came, in phone calls and letters, more attention than a published poem of mine has ever received. A blunt former classmate from college was dismissive: "I
could've done that," she said. An old girlfriend got back in touch.
Poet-friends wrote from across the country, and one from Switzer-
land. All this attention warmed my sonneteer's heart, there in frozen Ithaca, where I was beginning my second semester as poet-in-
residence at Cornell, and made me eager to get new work to Mr.
Moss.

But my mother died back in North Carolina, five weeks later,
and the subsequent months were a postmortem whirlwind. I finally
mailed him five poems on the morning of September 17, 1987, not
knowing that this news was in *The New York Times* that day: "Howard Moss, a poet who for almost 40 years was the poetry editor of

The New Yorker, died of cardiac arrest yesterday at St. Vincent's Hospital and Medical Center of New York. Mr. Moss was 65 years old."

I was shocked. He was years younger than my father, and had seemed so vigorous. Who could imagine *The New Yorker* without Mr. Moss editing and publishing its poems? And what about our just-begun relationship, and his hope that "Snow Goat" was the first of many poems of mine to appear in the magazine? As the obituary said, many prominent poets "published their early work with Mr. Moss," including Theodore Roethke, Richard Wilbur, Sylvia Plath, and James Dickey, whose poetry I adored.

Poor Howard Moss, obviously. What an unexpected and terrible loss. But also: poor me.

7.

As it happened, that sonnet was a one-off. I've never appeared in *The New Yorker* again, though not for lack of trying. I submitted to Howard Moss's successor twenty-one times over the next seventeen years; she rejected me every time, with a few vaguely friendly notes. (My teenage son, hearing the number of times I was told No, said, "It seems like you would've taken the hint, years ago.") In the 1990s, she lost three manuscripts. I've also submitted to the poetry editor who succeeded Mr. Moss's successor a few times; his last rejection began, "It was very pleased to have had the opportunity to read your new poems." (I wish somebody had proofread that form letter, and caught his initial "It" mistake.)

Would I like to be back in the pages of *The New Yorker*, despite the long hiatus? Absolutely. And yet: I do not think I will submit again. Not because of all those rejections, though I have indeed begun to take the hint. Not because I'm older, and it's time to let the younger writers have their day in the magazine. And not because unsolicited poetry submissions are handled online now, in an impersonal manner that precludes direct address to or contact with the editor.

No, the reason is this: I doubt I could improve on my single appearance in the magazine. It came about at least in part because of a personal contact with a generous old-school editor, whom I greatly admired. The poem he printed is one I can still stand by: it holds up as both debut and farewell, hello and goodbye, aloha. Am I the poetic version of the journeyman baseball player who labors in the minors for years, then has one longed-for game in the majors, then disappears back into the minors for the rest of his career? That's fine. It was a great cup of coffee. I'm happy with that metaphor and fate. And I still have a copy of my *New Yorker*, which I can pull out and leaf through, if I need or want to: for one week, way back in early 1987, I was a cartoon-sized part of the best that was being thought and said and written in America, and that temporary glory is plenty.

THE SMALLEST TALK:
ONE-LINE POEMS

1.

A one-line poem is not a longer poem condensed, a larger block of text whittled down to a single thin horizontal. It's not made in the manner Pound claims he wrote "In a Station of the Metro," reducing it—over the course of a year and a half—from thirty lines to a poem half that length to a haiku-like utterance. It doesn't work that way.

2.

Neither is a one-line poem incomplete, a forsaken first or last line waiting for the rest of the poem to show up, even if the rest of the poem is only the other half of an heroic couplet: it's a self-contained verbal universe, from which not a word can be shaken and to which not a word should be grafted.

3.

You don't set out to write a one-line poem. Rather, you have the usual sort of internal stirrings—an image, a phrase, a passage—and discover, while incubating that material, that it resists elaboration and keeps rounding itself down to a single line, one that takes hours or days or months or years to achieve precisely the right shape. The inspiration-irritation yields a single pearl.

MICHAEL McFEE   137

4.

Once you realize you're writing one, a one-line poem can be quite liberating, despite its obvious constrictions. You don't have to wonder how long it should be, as is often the case with poems not in a set form. You don't have to fret about enjambment: there will be none, since no other lines will emerge to be turned and broken down the page. You don't have to worry about punctuation at the end of the line: let it hang there, cantilevered, suggestive and unresolved, inviting the reader back into it, again and again.

No, the muse has rationed you one line, that's all, with a beginning, an end, and a few words between those termini. Now what? Can you make something worthwhile happen there, something intriguing and surprising and truly moving? How satisfying can that short journey be?

5.

A one-line poem, at its best, is a feat of true wit: when less successful, it's a mere cleverness, too easy and quick, good for a chuckle or a *hmmmm* but not genuinely evocative, thought-provoking, unforgettable.

6.

Early in the 1980s, I saw (or dreamed I saw: why would such a poet have been on TV, even then?) John Ashbery on the *Dick Cavett Show*. Cavett asked him to read a poem and Ashbery, taking only a few seconds, did:

The Cathedral Is

Slated for demolition.

As I recall, Cavett immediately jumped him: "Why is that a poem?" he challenged, or maybe he just asked, "Is that actually a poem?" I don't remember Ashbery's answer, but I do remember thinking that was a fair and honest question—and still do.

Was that when my obsession with one-line poems took root?

7.

A one-line poem is very difficult to read aloud or hear aloud, since it requires more words to set it up than are in the text itself: it may be the antithesis of poetry as an oral art.

8.

If "concentration is of the essence in poetry," as *Les Imagistes* claimed, is a one-line poem the most essential poem possible? Or would that quintessence be a one-word poem—if such a creature can actually exist, in any meaningful way?

It's certainly the most paper-wasteful poem possible, with much more white space than usual going uninked, the page barely saved from blankness.

9.

A one-line poem is not a prose poem, a little sentence or sentence fragment, a micro-paragraph: it is emphatically a poetic line, its diction and rhythm as intense and musical as in any good poem.

10.

"It is an interesting question," pronounces the *New Princeton Encyclopedia of Poetry and Poetics*, in its "monostich" entry, "whether a one-line poem is possible." Do "gnomes, epigrams, proverbs, and funerary inscriptions from the ancient world, both Cl. Gr. and Celtic," count? There's no way to say, since we don't know those writers' intentions—and authorial intent is critical to a genuine one-line poem: the poet must conceive of his material that way, must write it that way, and must mean for the audience to hear and/or read it that way. The true monostich is a product of deliberate pressure, not a casual or accidental creation: it is meant to resonate no less than a cathedral bell striking one o'clock. "The Delphic Oracle spoke thus," as the *NPEPP* says; and who are we to disagree with such a hefty authority?

11.

A one-line poem is subversive, an extreme lyric finger in the face of the epic or longwinded novel; and its audaciousness is no less an affront to the writer than to the reader. It's a prank knife pulled on what we expect a poem to look like, and be.

12.

I don't know where I found a copy of William Matthews's *An Oar in the Old Water*, that ugly harvest-gold chapbook published by The Stone in 1976, on what dusty used-bookstore shelf in what city. I don't remember when I bought it (sometime in the 1980s or early 1990s?), or when I first read it, or when it seized my imagination. But once it did, I was hooked on one-line poems, on the possibilities of such witty soulful brevity as

Silence

All bells hate their clappers

or

Physics

Is death curved, like the universe?

or

"To Thine Own Self Be True"

As if you had a choice

I only wish I could have talked with the author about one-line poems before he died, about how much fun those crafty little effusions are, about how challenging it is to try and get one right, as he did in these and in other beauties like "Sleep" or "Snow" or, especially, "Premature Ejaculation."

13.

A one-line poem depends on its title to work, but the title is not a separate line as such: it's the crucial initial note in the chord struck by the poem, and neither can work without the other.

14.

Fourteen one-line poems do not a sonnet make. But a series of one-line poems can develop an argument or present a scene or imply a story no less than a sonnet or any other form. Though self-sufficient, one-line poems depend on each other for context, they speak and echo across all that white space, and they benefit from the sorts of thematic and tonal juxtapositions that Matthews makes with twenty-four poems and three equal sections in *An Oar in the Old Water*.

15.

A one-line poem is harder to publish in a magazine than a really long poem, but the problem is similar: most editors are made nervous by extremes of concentration or discursiveness, fearing that the literary public will read the former too quickly and the latter not at all.

16.

A one-line poem is not just a joke, a mere one-liner or punchline, a wisecrack by a wiseacre—though it is not infrequently funny, if darkly so, and though it does rely, above all, on timing.

17.

A one-line poem is not a maxim or aphorism or Zen adage. It is, like all lyric poems, a showing and not a saying.

18.

On September 12, 2003, I e-mailed several dozen poets and asked if they'd written any one-line poems or could point me toward any good ones—I had my own private anthology, but wanted to expand it. Matthews's poems were often mentioned, and W. S. Merwin's

Elegy

Who would I show it to

was quoted more than any other. I didn't know that longwinded
Whitman had written one—

To Old Age

I see in you the estuary that enlarges and spreads itself grandly
    as it pours in the great sea.

—or that Yvor Winters had published a whole pamphlet of them,
The Magpie's Shadow, in 1922, including

A Deer

The trees rose in the dawn.

Mark Jarman summed up the general feeling about one-line
poems: "I can't think of anything harder to write."

19.

Poetry is already the smallest talk possible, the most compact
and deliberate and charged use of language. A one-line poem simply
takes that squeezing of the material as far as it can go on the page
and still be a poem. Such focus surrounded by such silence is like a
spiritual exercise, a prayer approaching the wordless word.

20.

Writing a one-line poem is a strangely impersonal act. There's
no room for digressive self-absorption, no time to develop a sus-

tained first-person point-of-view, no chance for sentimental lapses: you must get in and out so quickly that you simply don't have those luxuries. A one-line poem is a stone, not a mirror: it's a classical discipline, the most chiseled kind of epigrammatic writing. In such an abbreviated universe, your first word is already almost your last:

Her Name

Hello wet prayer that would not burn

PROOFS

Proofs may be my favorite stage in making a book.

It's not the writing of the book itself, which is ambiguous and protracted, the committing of poems year after year, often with no definite idea of how or if they'll fit together as a collection in the end. That process has its pleasures along the way, but they are fitful.

It's not necessarily the existence of the finished volume either, though holding that first copy in your hand is a triumphant moment worthy of champagne. But the initial flush can fade pretty quickly, especially when aided by lukewarm-to-negative reviews, if any.

For some obsessive reason, I always anticipate and enjoy reading the proofs of my forthcoming book, ready to mark its provisional pages with a red pen, comparing the intermediate version line for line with the original manuscript, reading aloud what I'd written in the same manner: patiently, painstakingly, deliberately. I made this book, I am the only one who will ever read it this way, I am savoring it in the privacy of my home and can take as long as I want to appreciate its verbal turns and dips and flourishes.

Proofs are the closest you'll get to manuscript again, the text illuminated by your restless hand.

Proofs have a lovely (and increasingly archaic) lingo. Galleys. Master proofs. Dead copy. Foul galleys.

The proofreader's shorthand and symbols are likewise charming and arcane. The unraveled ampersand of the delete sign. The octothorpe's simple grid, signifying "insert space." The backwards capital P of "begin new paragraph." The carets fulcruming sentences, adding commas or apostrophes or quotation marks. The alphabetical fractions that mean "insert em dash" or "insert en dash." The Latin *stet*, commanding: "Let it stand."

How satisfying, back in the 1970s and 1980s, when I worked as an editor for various publications and offices, to annotate the text in such a way that a third party—not me, not the author, but a never-seen professional typesetter called The Compositor—could understand it without my ever using an actual English word.

Proofs are the book's blueprints. In fact, a latter stage of proofs is called "bluelines," though they lack the intoxicating smell that rose off the big sheets of architectural drawings in the basement of the Six Associates firm in Asheville, as I watched blueprints slowly roll from the machines. Maybe that's why I like proofs so much, that old graphic association, those subterranean head-sick blues.

Proofs slow you down. They make you read with exaggerated care the text you created—line by line, phrase by phrase, word by word, syllable by syllable, letter by letter: they make you read what you wrote, not what you think you wrote.

Proofs are usually reviewed in solitude, as the work was created in solitude and will be experienced in solitude.

But some of my most enjoyable proofing happened when I was a graduate student on the staff of *Carolina Quarterly*, long before the computerized generation of texts and revisions. The poetry editor Rex McGuinn and I would sit down with a sheaf of page proofs and a stack of original manuscripts, and together we would crawl through the poems a final time. One of us would read the accepted poem aloud to the other, who was scrutinizing the proofs: the reader would pause between each word, spelling out any ambiguities, vocalizing punctuation marks and line breaks and any typographical quirks, all to ensure that the printed poem was as close to perfect as we could make it. That could take quite a while, especially with long poems like Fred Chappell's "Remembering Wind Mountain at Sunset": "Stanza break. Italics. Capital *I—saw—blackbird*, one word—*fighting—the—hawk*, comma, line break—capital H *He—whupped*, w-h-u-p-p-e-d—*his—hiney*, h-i-n-e-y—*with-a-pokeweed*, p-o-k-e-w-e-e-d—*stalk*, period, stanza break. End italics, back to Roman type. Capital A And—then—he—says, comma—capital N Now—how—you, line break—going—to—pay—me, question mark, space—capital I—says, note the terminal s—capital P Pay—you—doc, comma—you'll—just, line break—have—to—garnisheer, g-a-r-n-i-s-h-e-e-r—them—capital R Rest—capital W Wages, period, stanza break..."

Why did I cheerfully endure hour after hour of what must sound like verbal torture? It felt good and right to me. It felt like manual labor, which satisfies me. It felt like the ultimate way to honor the best and most concentrated use of language possible: by articulating one sound at a time.

And as Oscar Wilde correctly said: "A poet can survive everything except a typo."

"Proofs" was the chapter I consulted most in the old *Chicago Manual of Style*, back when I worked at Duke as an editorial assistant. These sentences came near the end, in the "Finished Book" entry: "When the folded sheets reach the bindery, one or two copies of the bound book from the first run are sent to the publisher's production department, where the book is checked for flaws in binding or assembling. Normally, neither author nor editor sees the book at this stage, but if they happen to be present they may be allowed to hold it for a while." Afterwards, must the newborn book be torn from their arms and returned to the nursery?

Proofs are still sent out by some journals and magazines. For single poems, it doesn't take long to compare the typeset version to the original. Sometimes there are small mistakes, or quibbles over corrected spelling or punctuation, but mostly it's a matter of examining the page headed "32 SOUTHERN REVIEW (Summer '01)—11-15x24(28)-Baskrvle 1-l.fl," then initialing/dating it and writing, "Fine."

Proofs are your last chance to get it right—really right, finally right, irreversibly right— in words. They are the ultimate revisions.

Proofs of poetry books are usually pretty much finished, given that they're printed from the tidy computer file you sent the publisher. Proofing them requires reining yourself in as you read, so that you don't scan too fast and assume everything is perfect, only to discover an indelible erratum once the finished book arrives.

I read the proofs of my seventh collection yesterday, and surprised myself with how much I enjoyed it. I laughed out loud. I nodded my head. I said, "Not bad." And I affixed red check after red check at the top of the page, signifying "No errors" literally but also somehow meaning, "Yes. This was good when I wrote it, and it's still good, here in the company of other good poems."

I should probably be embarrassed by such egotism, but I'm not. Today I mail the marginally corrected proofs back to the press, and the next time I see my book it'll be as the finished, bound volume to be held and sold in bookstores. By then, my self-satisfied proofing stage will be long gone, and my pride in what I wrote and how I wrote it may be edging toward indifference, or possibly despair— not simply "Why did I write this, and why did I publish it?" but also "Can I ever write anything this good again?"

≡

Proofs are a sort of chrysalis, the latter stages when something's stirring inside. What will emerge from that wordy cocoon?

ЗС

Proofs of a prose book are the most difficult to deal with, as I discovered with my first collection of essays.

When writing a poem, there comes a point when I'm clearly done tinkering: the poem is either complete or unsalvageable, and I know it's time to move on. But with an essay, the tweaking and finessing never ends: I can always improve a phrase or tighten a sentence or (typical poet) find a way to polish the prose to a slightly brighter sheen. Not that this necessarily improves the piece, but it does make it sound a bit better, and that fine-tuning process seems like it could go on forever.

The same impulse applies to the proofing stage. Though most of the copyedited sentences in the several hundred pages of *The Napkin Manuscripts* seemed fine, too many others hit my ear slightly wrong, and drew my red pen toward them, whispering, "Make us better—you know you want to!" I had to resist that siren call, and try to make only the minimum essential marks: this was no time for rewriting. But it was hard not to think that, with another week or month or two, it could've been a more eloquent book.

○

Proofs are like grading yourself, the corrective bloody marks in either margin showing how you could and should improve.

lc

Proofs require microscopically attentive reading, which can be tedious after a while. But every vocation has its tedium, and one measure of the rightness of your calling is your willingness to endure its tiresome aspects. That's one reason I left architecture: I didn't have the patience to suffer the relentless back-and-forth grind of long-term design projects. But I've never minded the detailed solitary negotiations that writing requires, or the proofing of the writing, which starts as soon as I put a single word on a single page and then reconsider it.

Rough drafts are the foundation work for later proofs.

caps

Proofs impose a welcome deadline. In practical terms, they have to be returned by such a date, even by such a time, or else the whole production process is held up and publication delayed. In creative terms, if there weren't a firm date for the manuscript's return, it would be tempting to keep fiddling with the text long beyond the point where such fiddling is actually helpful.

Dr. Johnson: "When a man knows he is to be hanged in a fortnight, it concentrates his mind wonderfully."

tr

"Proofs," according to the *American Heritage Dictionary*, are "trial sheets of printed material that are made to be checked and corrected." That first adjective captures the trial-and-error nature of writing, from drafts at the desk through proofs to finished book.

Proof is from the Latin verb *probare*, to test, which is from *probus*, good. I like those aspects of proofing, too: it's a near-final testing of the text, to see if it's really good enough to send out into the world.

sp

God proofed His work, and saw that it was good.

stet

Proofs are the real proof that I'm a writer: they prove it to me, which is what really matters day to day. They make me want to go on, to sit down at the desk with pen and as-yet-unmarked paper, to prove myself again and again and again.

ANTHOLOGIZING

a.

An anthology is like a library, its contents organized not by the Dewey Decimal or Library of Congress system, but by principles of the editor's own devising, designed to please and educate its readers, to delight and instruct. It is, like any library anywhere, a distillation and arrangement of available material, its poems surrounded by the white space that embodies a library's silence, attentiveness, and inward joy.

b.

Poetry abounds in fine etymologies, but the best may be that of "anthology," from the Greek for "flower-gathering." Down to its linguistic roots, an anthology is a collection of flowers, a bouquet, a selection of the best blooms in the poetic garden, carefully cut and arranged and presented to an appreciative reader by a discerning anthologist.

On the one hand, this is a great convenience. You don't have to comb through thousands of individual books of poems to find the most dazzling ones: Donald Hall or Rita Dove or some other editor has already done that work for you, and gathered the results into a single volume that takes up much less space on the shelf. This is why anthologies are so widely used in schools at all levels, where most of us first encounter poetry in its anthologized form: as handy, portable, relatively cheap volumes, with each poem's worth confirmed by its inclusion in the collection, or at least acknowledged in a way that the millions of other non-anthologized verses are not. These poems must be all-stars, part of a legendary constellation:

who wouldn't want to read them, or write one of them and achieve a kind of immortality by association?

On the other hand: though an anthology may indeed be a useful volume, saving time and money and energy, it is also—by its very nature—a misrepresentation. No anthology can be truly comprehensive: it must be a culling of the abundant blossoming, one person's selection from a very large field of flowers. It's not the choice you would have made, and it's certainly not the choice the author would have made, if indeed the poet could choose a dozen from many hundreds of beloved literary children and offer them up for display. An anthology should propel us from its collection or selection, however intriguing or unsatisfying, to the actual books of the poets themselves, to the library or bookstore shelves where we can read the poems in the context of individual volumes and discover other unanthologized beauties—though we're also likely to find plenty of weaker work that deserves to be buried in a *Collected Poems*, if it should be in print at all.

c.

Children are very familiar with anthologies. The Bible is a wild anthology, one some of us heard from a very early age, again and again, though we probably didn't think of it as described by the *Princeton Encyclopedia of Poetry and Poetics*: "a heterogeneous collection of Jewish (Hebrew) and Christian (Greek) texts written over more than a millennium." Hymnals are also anthologies—that's one of the archaic definitions of "anthology" in the *Oxford English Dictionary*. And we were often read to out of anthologies, collections of children's poems and stories that we heard and reheard and found delightful: there's no lovelier sight and sound than a parent reading to a child, is there?

And then, a bit later, the hormones hit, and we started listening to rock & roll on the radio or LP records, each album offering its dozen or so black roses, later reconfigured as a *Greatest Hits* collection, a *Best of* anthology...

Is this stretching the notion of "anthologizing" too thin? Not really. It's a basic human urge, this selective collecting, and it's particularly central to our mutual literary enterprise, to reading and then sharing what Matthew Arnold called culture, "the best which has been thought and said in the world."

d.

Every reader is anthologizing, all the time, and should be. If you're making your way through a book of poetry with the attention it deserves—slowly, receptively, stopping to mouth the words aloud, rereading and savoring a poem, penciling notes in the margins— you'll find that some of the poems give you more pleasure than others, for whatever reason. And those poems become part of the mental anthology that you always carry around, savoring them privately, sometimes sharing your enthusiasms with others, and never quite forgetting the work that left its mark on your ear and eye, your heart and mind. If you were assembling an anthology for publication, you'd want to include x from this anthology (side note: anthologies are often gathered out of other anthologies), or y from that magazine, or z from an individual volume. This is natural, and this is healthy. It's like a literary mix-tape or -CD, where you say to a friend: *Here's what excites and moves me; I hope you like it, too.*

It doesn't matter if your private anthology is ever actually published: the fact is, every reader is an anthologist, listening for good poems, considering new ones as well as old friends, always looking to be surprised by those concentrated verbal worlds that have spun into view for the first time or returned for another appreciative viewing.

e.

One of Robert Pinsky's pieces of advice for young writers is: "Make your own personal anthology." This excellent exercise requires you to (1) read widely and carefully; (2) select thirty to fifty of your absolute favorite poems; (3) type each one of them out—a lot to ask, in these online copy-and-paste days, but a great manual way to learn things about how the poem's words work on the page; and (4) figure out how to organize them.

I've used this assignment a few times with my students, and added a fifth requirement: (5) write an introduction to your anthology that gives the reader an idea of why you chose and arranged as you did. The results have been most enlightening, for anthologist and teacher. Could and should "Anthologizing" be a course in creative writing programs, at whatever level, an extended and very instructive lesson in how this corner of literature's garden is tended?

f.

Making your own personal anthology is more than a mere exercise: it's an extension and an affirmation of your life as a reader. Such a collection is, as Rachel Hadas puts it, "a window into one person's taste, memory, and emotions; it amounts to a compressed literary memoir." How curious, the idea that one's memoir could be written by other writers; and yet, at its best, how attractive and true.

The making of a personal anthology is an ongoing—indeed, a lifelong—process. "What do I need to become an anthologist?" asks Randall Jarrell. "Taste... Nothing expresses and exposes your taste so completely—nothing is your taste so nearly—as that vague final treasury of the *really* best poems that grows in your head all your life." His "treasury" is right on the money, the idea that we readers can carry valued and valuable poems in our heads to the end of our days, words that, to us and our taste, are priceless.

g.

A good anthology is like a good museum, each poem a memorable work of art displayed in a gallery to its best advantage, to please and inspire us in ways that, ultimately, can't quite be articulated.

h.

"Poetry redeems from decay the visitations of the divinity in man," said Shelley, an enduring pronouncement about poetry, mostly for the first part: "poetry redeems from decay," it saves something on the page that would otherwise decompose, disintegrate, disappear. It becomes a way of remembering things that would otherwise be forgotten.

That's one reason I have all my students memorize and recite poems. By committing a poem to memory, by taking it into your mind and body, by speaking it aloud instead of merely reading it silently, you have made it physically a part of you; and if you memorize several more, a dozen, fifty, a hundred, you become a walking anthology, able to speak a poem at any time, for whatever reason.

Anthologizing serves a similar function, if it's not quite as radical as memorizing: by selecting, and copying, and thinking about a poem that's special to you, and arranging it with other such poems, you have helped redeem it from decay and oblivion, which is most gratifying to Mnemosyne, the goddess of memory and mother of the nine muses.

i.

Don't we all compile a secret Anthology of Underappreciated Writers? Mine features Robert Francis, not just for his subtle and marvelous lyric poems but also for *The Satirical Rogue on Poetry*, a slim collection of eighty-four very brief essays, sly and impish and spot-on. The "Poets on Poetry" series at the University of Michigan Press collected that book and further roguish pronouncements by Francis in *Pot Shots at Poetry*, which includes a piece called "Anthologists," a quietly radical take on the relationship of anthologizing to canon-making, on the difference between anthologists and critics.

"Anthologists are by derivation flower gatherers," Francis begins, "but flower gathering hardly suggests the seriousness of their pursuit. It would be more accurate to liken them to bees, whose seriousness and industry are proverbial... For after the critics have decided who the real poets are—the pure, the important, the immortal—the anthologists come along with rather a different answer. They are less interested in poet than poem; and less interested in the pedigree of a poem than in its readability. If critics are aristocrats, writing for the few about the few, anthologists are usually democrats, writing for the many and hoping for a good sale."

I know of no higher compliment than to say: I wish I'd written that.

j.

Are there too many anthologies in print? Probably so, especially Houghton Mifflin's annual Best American series, which by now includes not merely the *Best American Short Stories* and *Best American Poetry* and *Best American Essays*, but also the *Best American Science and Nature Writing*, *Best American Sports Writing*, and *Best American Non-Required Reading*, whatever that is. The persistence of this genre or sub-genre shows that at least one publisher believes there's an audience for it.

Does this mean that readers have gotten lazier and want somebody else to pick the best for them, or that there are so many books published, nobody can keep up? Possibly so. And yet, where's the harm?—unless anthologies are keeping readers from actually buying the books in which the work originally appeared.

Some poetry teachers argue against the typical reliance on anthologies in the classroom, instead calling for the use of individual volumes of poetry, which would benefit both the press and the author. Unfortunately, that can get expensive for the student and exhausting for the teacher, and it doesn't provide the historical and aesthetic range that's particularly instructive for my lower-level undergraduates. Or am I just lazy, too, and an enabler of other lazy readers?

k.

Not all anthologists gather "great" poems. Take D. B. Wyndham Lewis and Charles Lee, who edited *The Stuffed Owl: An Anthology of Bad Verse*, which is exactly what the subtitle says it is: a collection of outstanding "Bad Verse" from three centuries of English poetry, unintentional literary howlers that are most entertaining. What makes this book a comic masterpiece, and the funniest anthology ever published, is exactly what makes the Norton anthologies so dull: the introduction, the head- and footnotes, and (believe it or not) the index.

The editors thoughtfully provide a prefatory selection of Hors d'Oeuvres and a concluding section of Postprandials, selected lines from some of the best Bad Verse, such as "Her smile was silent as the smile on corpses three hours old." They also include such useful biographical details as "The duchess was fantastic in dress as in writing, wore many face-patches, and was virtuous to the point of ill-breeding." But the best part of the book was added for the second edition: "It is hoped," say Lewis and Lee, "that serious students will welcome the addition of a Subject Index," with such tongue-in-cheek entries as "Englishman, his heart a rich rough gem that leaps and strikes and glows and yearns" or "Immortality, hope of, distinguishes man from silk-worm" or "Manure, adjudged a fit subject for the Muse" or "Oxygen, glorious, God's."

All this, plus eight witty illustrations by Max Beerbohm, including "Walt Whitman, inciting the Bird of Freedom to soar." As Daffy Duck would say, it is to laugh. And it is to remind us readers and writers and editors of poetry not to take ourselves too seriously, always a healthy lesson.

1.

Some anthologies, alas, are cemeteries, each poem a gravestone to an outdated idea or taste. Such gatherings are not merely mortal: they can be actively anti-immortal.

Many anthologies are period pieces: their pages may not be graves but they do have a musty antique smell when we open them a decade or a century later.

However, it's good that a fellow human went to the trouble of anthologizing, once upon a time. And the poems themselves, the few really fine ones, survive and endure, waiting to be read, rediscovered, resurrected by an appreciative reader.

m.

As an undergraduate would-be poet, I became smitten with anthologies, in particular the 1973 edition of *The Norton Anthology of Modern Poetry*. Now I find it fairly annoying, with its pretentious headnotes and unnecessary footnotes, but as an English major and young writer, it was the epitome of culture to me: a tall blue block of a book, a poetic Holy Scriptures—actually printed on opaque Bible paper—whose Genesis was Whitman, whose Exodus was Dickinson, whose prophets were Yeats and Pound and Eliot, and whose New Testament good news came from Roethke, Bishop, Lowell, and other writers born even closer to my own birthdate. When I was really giddy, I fancied that I would someday become the tip of this poetry iceberg, the last poet in some future edition, the gleaming blade of the cutting edge. (Side note: That's often the least reliable part of a chronological anthology, the most contemporary writers—the ones whose parentheses are only half-full, the post-dash date of death not yet filled in.)

As a fledgling haunter of used bookstores, I headed straight for the poetry section first, always checking out the anthologies, the ways that different editors had conceived to take a core sample of the incomprehensibly huge planet of poetry. Pretty much any Faber or Oxford or Penguin book of poetry made the Anglophile in me swoon. Over the years I have gathered, and still have on my shelves, anthologies whose poems are focused on and organized around such topics as baseball, sports and games, music, movies, visual art, birds, Christmas, work, cars, friendship, love, marriage, war, God, Greek myths, Shakespeare, erotic poetry, cowboy poetry, light verse, and— one of my favorites, though it does include prose—Drink, Drinkers, and Drinking. And I keep buying anthologies, including the darling little Everyman's Library Pocket Poets volumes, with their clever dustjackets and decorative endpapers and silk ribbon markers.

And of course there are dozens, hundreds, thousands of other approaches to anthologizing poetry, not only by theme or subject but by date, by nation or region or state or city, by—well, you imagine it, and it's probably already been done.

But that didn't stop me from doing it myself.

n.

I've edited two anthologies of contemporary North Carolina literature. That might sound like a mighty narrow way to slice the literary pie, but in fact the Tar Heel state produced many fine writers in the last few decades of the twentieth century, when I was reading their new books closely. There was (I knew) plenty to choose from, there were (I believed) readers who wanted to read it, and there was (I hoped) a publisher who would want to bring out such a collection: the University of North Carolina Press.

The first of these anthologies was born out of irritation, possibly jealousy—feelings that should not be undervalued as spurs to getting things done. The 1980s had seen a startling outburst of first-rate writing in our state, what Fred Chappell later called a "literary efflorescence," and I had spent most of that decade reviewing those books in a local weekly magazine and on a local NPR station, trying to pay them the kind of attention they weren't getting in the national media, though most were being published by national houses and presses. When these writers were getting noticed, it was usually the fiction writers—which was fine, some of my best friends were and are fiction writers, but as a poet that started to grate on me. There were plenty of excellent North Carolina poets doing wonderful work: why were they and their poems not being noticed?

Once UNC Press published *The Rough Road Home: Stories by North Carolina Writers*, in 1992, my fate was sealed. I liked that book, and its focus on local short fiction, but I knew it was only half the story. I wanted to make a companion volume featuring contemporary North Carolina poetry, to show that it could and should be enjoyed by any serious reader who also enjoyed novels and short stories. And though I didn't consciously think about it at first, I wanted to become an anthologist, the editor of a volume whose poems were handpicked by me, one that would really show how it should be done.

o.

There are pleasures to be had in making an anthology to be published as a book. One is dreaming up the idea for your collection. Another is convincing a press to say, *Okay, we'll publish this.* And a very major pleasure, a season of happiness, is the sweet time when you're reading and reading and reading, thousands of poems in hundreds of books, all sprawled around your desk or chair as you re-read and re-read and re-read, picking the choicest fruit, making lists or piles of "YES!" and "Maybe" and "no," trying to decide which poems might, then could, then should, then must make the cut into the final gathering—all of this is fun, a reader's honeymoon, and we all do it when reading and judging books.

But then come the griefs. The first is that your selection is far too large, so you must cut poems or poets that you really wanted to include in your anthology. (Side note: this excision will come back to haunt you later, guaranteed.) The second grief is that the press has "helpful" suggestions that ruin the beautiful balance of what you've made, like, say, insisting that a certain famous writer be included in your book because she is nationally known and will sell copies, though you insist that (1) she isn't really a poet, (2) she isn't really a very good poet, (3) she isn't really a North Carolinian, though she maintains a residence in the state, and (4) her presence in your anthology won't actually sell more copies.

They win. You lose. Other losses follow, including the payment of permission-to-reprint fees by the editor (not the press), which can lead to some strange negotiations. Here's one I had with a major New York publisher—I'd written three or four letters, with no response, and finally got the rights and licensing department on the phone.

Me: "This is Michael McFee, in Chapel Hill, North Carolina. I've written you about an anthology I'm editing, of North Carolina poetry—"

Guy, cutting me off: "Yeah, yeah, I know who you are." Silence.

Me, after waiting: "Well, then, as you may remember, I'd like to use six poems from a book you published—"

Guy, cutting me off again: "Six hundred dollars."

Me: "Sir, as you may remember, this book is being published by a not-for-profit university press—"

Guy, cutting me off yet again: "Okay, three hundred dollars."

Me, continuing: "—a university press, and I am a part-time teacher paying for reprint fees from my own pocket—"

Guy, cutting me off one more time: "Okay, jeez! One-fifty. Final offer."

However, most presses and most authors were much more gracious, and the paperwork got done, and the anthology was finally published, by the University of North Carolina Press, in 1994, as *The Language They Speak Is Things to Eat: Poems by Fifteen Contemporary North Carolina Poets.*

p.

The anthology sold well (for a university press), the few reviews were friendly, the book got adopted for a college course or two (and continues to be used, now and then), but some unhappy readers surfaced. The poets I couldn't or didn't include were understandably miffed. I also heard that, at a writers' conference I couldn't attend, one of the state's most venerable literary statesmen stood up and said that any anthology of North Carolina poems not including at least a hundred poets wasn't a real sampling of the poetry being written in our state.

He was right: my anthology was different from other regional anthologies, and a critique of their approach. As I wrote in the introduction, "Rather than offering quick tastes of many poets, then snatching readers off to another dish in the poetry buffet once they've found something they like, this anthology offers generous servings of fewer poets....Just as fiction writers may need ten or fifteen pages in order to fully develop a story, poets benefit from a more substantial sampling of their work, something more comprehensive than a single lyric poem, however delicious."

My implicit critique of Norton anthologies: Use no footnotes, and move the prose about the poets to the back of the book, where readers can look at it or not. The poems are the point.

Did I make mistakes with *The Language They Speak*? Definitely. But mostly I'm still pretty proud of the book I made from other poets' poems. Would I ever do another poetry anthology? I doubt it. That may well be a young person's calling: it takes a certain swagger and energy to do it right, and such vigor as I still possess needs to go into my own writing. But I'm glad that other editors are still plucking and arranging the poetic flowers in new ways, because to do so is a public way of reading and re-reading and thinking about what Coleridge called "the best words in the best order."

q.

Do some anthologists publish work by their friends, their students, their colleagues, their mentors, their lovers, themselves? To be sure: it has always been thus.

Does that matter? Not as long as the work fits the parameters of the anthology and actually deserves to be in there, along with the other work lacking personal connections.

I included my own poetry in *The Language They Speak*, because it met the requirements and seemed worthy of inclusion. At the time, that felt like the right thing to do, and also like a reward to myself for all the labor that went into the book. Now, looking back, it seems a vain mistake; or maybe it's those youthful poems that pain me, and that author photo with the 1980s haircut and mustache...

r.

A favorite anthology is like a favorite cookbook, a collection of thoroughly tested and tasted recipes that have been proven to work, to satisfy, to delight. We know we can go back to them again and again, and be fulfilled.

s.

Another worthwhile thing about anthologizing: it can help you learn to put your own books of poetry together. The process is pretty much identical: you have a number of poems written over a number of years, you choose the ones that seem strongest and work together well, and you arrange them in a way that makes emotional sense. The poems may tell a story, even if the narrative is buried; they may pursue a motif or technical concern; they may cohere around a subject or character or thematic center—whatever it is they seem to be doing, you try to put one poem next to the other in a way that strengthens each and develops a coherent whole. Poems write themselves together while written apart, and your job—as editor of an anthology or of your own poems—is to discover those connections and make them into a meaningful pattern for the reader of your book.

Poets have different degrees of obsessiveness about the "capital-D" Design of their "capital-B" Book. Though readers may skip around in their collections, plucking what they fancy from those poem-gardens and not sitting down and reading the volumes straight through, we writers hope that attention will be paid to the order we devise. William Matthews was passionate about sequencing the poems in his individual volumes; other poets are more casual. A colleague and I were once trying to figure out the order of the poems in *Briefings*, by A. R. Ammons, and came up with an elaborate pattern of dark/light, death/life, etc./etc.: when we phoned Archie to find out if this was true, he said, "Well, that's very interesting, but I just arranged the poems alphabetically by first line." (Almost: he shrewdly moved one of his best poems, "The City Limits," which begins "When you consider the radiance," to the very end of the book, placing it after six poems starting with W's or Y's.)

The same principle—random, yet surprisingly evocative and effective—was used by Seamus Heaney and Ted Hughes in their 1984 poetry anthology *The Rattle Bag*, preserving an "unexpectedness," as they call it, that the book's contents might not otherwise possess.

I fall somewhere in between Matthews and Ammons. I do a preliminary winnowing of my poems, and build stacks of strong yes / probably yes / possibly yes poems, which I spread out on a big table. Then I spend hours walking around the poetry, making and changing groupings, putting different poems next to each other like different colors in a painting or different notes in a chord, experimenting, reconfiguring, trying to figure out the essence of what I've written and the best way to present it. Sometimes I know where I want the book to start or where I want it to end, sometimes I know certain poems that need to be together (or far apart), but in most cases I make sense of it as I go—exactly as I did with the anthologies, exactly as I do with every poem I write, where I have a beginning or a trigger but never know exactly where the words will take me. "No surprise for the writer, no surprise for the reader," as Frost says.

t.

In graduate school, I discovered—by happy accident, not design, the best way—W. H. Auden's prose book *A Certain World*. In so doing, I discovered the genre of the commonplace book, a personal miscellany of whatever words seem interesting to the compiler, along with any notes or comments he wishes to add. It's an informal journal of one's reading, and one's response to it: a commonplace book is like Pinsky's poetry anthology challenge, though it can also include prose of all kinds, quotes, overheard talk, or whatever catches one's eye and ear. *A Certain World* is a delight, playful and serious and surprising throughout. Auden read very widely, and—though a certifiable snob—his taste was quite eclectic. There are several hundred categorical entries in *A Certain World*, from "Acronyms" to

"World, End of the." Under "Names, Proper," Auden says, "Proper names are poetry in the raw. Like all poetry they are untranslatable. Someone who is translating into English a German novel, the hero of which is named *Heinrich*, will leave the name as it is; he will not Anglicize it into *Henry*." He follows this opening commentary with nine pages of quotes about names, including this gem from Thoreau: "With knowledge of the name comes a distincter recognition and knowledge of the thing."

It might seem peculiar and archaic to take the time and trouble to copy out fine passages of writing, to make a personal anthology of memorable words. But it's important to figure out a way of responding—regularly and thoughtfully—in words, to words, instead of simply reading something and forgetting it.

u.

Every editor of a magazine or journal is also anthologizing, reading through heaps of material, rejecting most of it (side note: surprising how easy that can be, when reading in context), setting aside some favorites, and then selecting a worthy handful for the next issue. This process can take weeks, months, years, and it's a far cry from the leisurely reading of poems for sheer pleasure, but finally it's the same thing: you make your way through piles of poem-blooms that have been dumped on your editorial table, and you select the most eye- and ear- and nose-catching for the next bouquet you will share with the world, arranging them next to each other in the most effective way.

v.

Robert Graves once wrote, "A well-chosen anthology is a complete dispensary of medicine for the more common mental disorders, and may be used as much for prevention as cure." I think that's praise, though I'm not sure.

Mrs. Robert Graves once received a letter that said, "An anthology is like all the plums and orange peel picked out of a cake." I think that's bad, but, again, I'm not positive.

When anthologies and anthologists are thought or written about, which is not often, they're usually regarded—like publishers—with suspicion, distrust, or bemusement. e.e. cummings had an acid epigram about Louis Untermeyer, a prolific anthologist whose *Treasury of Great Poems* was one of the most widely-read collections of English-language poetry for many years, concluding: "he sold the many on the few / not excluding mr u."

However, I do admire Mr U for once saying, "The purpose of an anthology must always be to arouse an interest rather than to satisfy a curiosity. If it brings its owners nearer the source, it will have fulfilled its prime function."

w.

Nicholson Baker's 2009 novel, *The Anthologist*, entertaining as it was, didn't do much for the public image of anthologists. The title character is a slightly unhinged out-of-favor poet who's trying to finish the introduction to his new anthology, but—for various personal and professional reasons—he simply can't get it done. The book is a series of eccentric but hilarious and often insightful digressions about poetry and literary culture, and especially about yearning for order in art and life and love; but (true to the narrator's avoidance of the task at hand) only rarely does the novel have much to do with actually being an anthologist or putting together an anthology.

One passage that does:

> You're determined that this is going to be a real anthology. This isn't going to be one of those anthologies where you sample it and think, Now why is that poem there? No, this is going to be an anthology where every poem you alight on and read, you say to yourself, Holy God *dang*, that is good. That is so good, and so twisty, and so shadowy, and so chewy, and so boomerangy, that it requires the forging of a new word for

beauty. *Rupasnil*. Beauty. *Rupasnil*. It's so good that as soon as you start reading the poem with your eyes you know immediately that you have to restart again reading it in a whisper to yourself so that you can really hear it. So good that you want to set it to musical notes of your own invention.

But as the narrator says, few poems reach that level of *rupasnil*, and so must be cut. In fact, he muses, weren't most of them included because of one fine stanza, or—honestly—one sublime line? He goes on to run his idea into the ground, as usual, reducing what's good about anthologized poems to "shockingly great" individual words. "But of course that's not going to work," he concludes. "That's just a bunch of disembodied words from great poems. And that's when you realize you're not an anthologist."

x.

The narrator of Baker's novel says that his forthcoming anthology of poetry, *Only Rhyme*, "would of course define me as an anthologist—i.e., as a lost soul who turned in despair to the publishing of other people's work, like old Oscar Williams." This comes near the end of a 243-page novel, and by that point we know it to be true of the speaker, who is comically adrift and desperate.

But is it true of anthologists in general? Are they all lost souls and lapsed writers who, in their lostness, turned to the publishing of other people's work? Is an editor's relationship to the anthologized work necessarily parasitic, feeding off those living host-poems while contributing nothing to their survival?

Or can it be, at its best, symbiotic, an arrangement mutually beneficial to both?

y.

The first essay in James Dickey's collection of criticism, *Babel to Byzantium: Poets and Poetry Now*, is called "In the Presence of

Anthologies." "The *raison d'être* of the anthology," Dickey says, about halfway through,

> is only secondarily to indicate trends, groups, schools, and periods, or to show what the young are writing, or what the old have written at different times, under different cultural conditions, or to demonstrate what Oscar Williams considers to be *A Treasury of Great Poems*. It is not to present a reflection of "the sensibility of an era" as seen in the eyes of its editors, or, more fragmentarily, in those of its poets. It is to lead readers to the poets on their home ground, their own books, where they present their worlds as fully and deeply as they are able.

That's a fine geographical image: anthologies should lead readers to the poets' own books, the "home ground" where their work is rooted, the world of words they've made there. The flowers in an anthologist's bouquet may look quite lovely together, but that's not their native place: though it requires more effort to do so, there's often a deeper pleasure to be taken back at the poems' source.

z.

An anthology, its etymology reminds us, is a metaphorical bouquet of poetic flowers. I have also suggested that a worthy anthology is like a library, a museum, or a cookbook, while a weak anthology is like a cemetery. Surely there are many other images for what anthologies can be, and for what we anthologists should and should not do when anthologizing.

In the end, a really good anthology is like a really good party, the editor its host, the poems its special guests, all talking to each other—and to you, a visitor at the poetry party and part of the conversation, the best of those best-of words lingering afterwards in your mouth and mind, as you head back home, word-tipsy, satisfied.

5.

POETS AS NOVELISTS

At a writers' conference many years ago, I heard a poet (who had written one novel) say, "Poets write novels in order to be considered successful. Novelists write poems in order to be considered artists." This did not please the fiction writers in the room.

I have several poet friends who, after writing and publishing excellent poetry for years, said they turned to writing fiction because they wanted a bigger audience. They quite reasonably yearned for more readers than poetry attracts, though literary fiction has a much smaller audience than the worst TV show or movie.

I tried to write a novel once. I went to a writers' retreat for a week, and in solitude wrote more than 100 pages of something that, on the page, looked like fiction: it was written in sentences and paragraphs and chapters, it had characters and some plot, it made a promising stack of paper. But it wasn't really fiction. Why? Because I couldn't leave the language alone. I'd write a good page or two, but then, instead of moving on with the story, I'd go back and improve what I'd written, pruning and tightening and polishing the diction until each sentence was a beautiful but independent string of words, disappearing into itself. The novel went nowhere. There was too much poetic attention to sound, not enough narrative flow-through or momentum. When it came to fiction, I was a proseur.

That week, I learned what I probably already knew: I encounter the world through language, image, measure, verbal pressure. By nature and practice, I'm a writer of poems, however small my audience may be, if I have an audience at all, besides myself. My texts are concentrated, not elaborated; as a poet-friend metaphorizes it, "I'm a sprinter, not a distance runner." Others are wired to write stories and novels, and I bet they'd do it whatever the size of their reading public: it's what they're good at, it's what they love, it's what they can't not do. There may be poets who are equally gifted as novelists, and vice versa, but my eyes and ears have rarely beheld such literary griffins.

NOVELISTS AS POETS

The less said, the better.

MIDDLING

Most poets get along fine with two names, first and last. Professionally, that's all we need, and we only get called by our last names when being reviewed, should that ever happen.

A few sublime poets have ascended to the heaven of one name. Dante. Shakespeare. Milton. In English, that means surname only, no given name needed.

Almost all of us have middle names, but they rarely get pressed into literary service, because they're so, well, middling. Typical. Uneventful. Some poets employ initials that distinguish them from the pack—A. E., D. H., T. S., e. e., W. H., among the moderns—but even that approach is unusual, as is first name + middle initial + last name.

Are we missing an opportunity here? Did all those Victorian tripleheaders know something we don't? True, many of their middle names aren't that interesting—Taylor, Waldo, Allan, Charles, Butler, to take a sample from one end of the nineteenth century to the other—but some had an undeniable panache and added welcome syllables to their bylines. "Bysshe" has a dishy sound, and somehow it seems part of Shelley's identity, especially that terminal *ssh*. "Gabriel" is de facto archangelic, and a nice trumpeting in the middle of one of the fanciest names in English poetry. And "Carlos" introduces an unexpected *olé* into what would otherwise be one of the dullest authorial handles ever, William Williams.

Fond as I am of a middle-name crow (though with a terminal e) and a saint (Vincent) among twentieth century poets, my three favorites go back to the golden age of intermezzo nomenclature. Who can resist Walter Landor, whose violent "Savage" hints at the darkness under his lyrical grace? Or John Whittier, whose eco-hippie "Greenleaf" seems just right for a poet so devoted to the rural and natural world? Or that once-obscure Jesuit whose extra-vowel "Manley" brings vigor to the somewhat bland Gerard Hopkins, embodying the sprung and springy rhythms of his verse?

Though it would be fun to change my pallid "Alan" to something more colorful, I can't think what it would be. As all poets know, finding the perfect title is really difficult. It's better to have a middle name ignored than snickered at.

SELECTED

Every individual book of poems is a "selected poems," in that the volume is a selection of poems written by the author over a certain period, a picking of the best available texts from a larger body of poetry, or a choosing of the ones that work best when juxtaposed and sequenced and gathered together into a larger whole. Which means that every book of poems is a kind of anthology, where the writer is also the editor, plucking attractive flowers from his private, uncut garden and making a bouquet for the reader. (Wouldn't it be interesting to give the same stack of poems to a dozen poets, and to see the very different books that could be made from identical material?)

Of course, there are volumes actually titled *Selected Poems*, in which the author reviews his earlier slim books of poetry and picks the work that has aged well, making a new gathering of highlights as well as a new category of "didn't make the cut," those older published poems that weren't quite memorable enough to invite to the *Selected Poems* party, now left to languish unnoticed in a dim corner. Sometimes poets and publishers add a "New" section to such a volume, a prefatory or benedictory offering of more recent work by the writer, a sort of Coming Attractions for the next book he might make. It's like a print version of a public reading, where the poet shares representative work from his volumes but also mixes in a few freshly-written poems, to show he's still got poetic game.

The days of the huge *Collected* or *Complete Poems*—those massive biblio-doorstops, confirming the author's Major Poet status—may be waning: they're costly to produce and to purchase, and the postmodern literary landscape is less hospitable to such verbal monuments. Which is fine, even appropriate. By its very nature, poetry is selective and not comprehensive. Every poem, in its writing and its revising, is a matter of selection, compression, and concentration, as the writer winnows language of its chaff. Few poets ever publish an actual *Selected Poems*, but every working poet is making one, line by choice line, word by select word.

UNCOLLECTED

I used to hate the idea of posthumous volumes of uncollected work, the poetry that Bishop or Larkin or Plath never published during their lifetimes: why gather, and then present to the public, poems that they didn't deem worthy of preserving in print? It seemed a ghoulish money-grubbing scheme, trading on the fame of the dead.

But my feelings may be changing, the older I get. Not that I think my own uncollected or unpublished work should ever see the light of day once I'm permanently in the dark: honestly, who would care? Not that I think every major poet's unprinted verse should be exhumed: I'm still all for suppressing juvenilia, since none of us should be held responsible for the apprentice words we wrote when at the mercy of hormonal muses. Not that I think a dead poet should necessarily usurp the increasingly precious shelf space that could go to a young, promising, living writer.

However, I know very well how fickle and unpredictable a poem's place in the world can be. I've written good poems that never found a home in a magazine, when lesser poems did, for whatever editorial reason; as a result, the unchosen eventually fell out of favor with their author, and got set aside, and were never collected with others into a book. When I'm going through my very thick stack of The Unpublished and Possibly Unpublishable, occasionally I'm pleasantly surprised by things I wrote years ago, and wonder why I removed them from circulation, and (if I'm in a really optimistic mood) wish that others might see and hear these words I worked so hard on: for a few days at least, I was devoted to these lines and stanzas, and getting them just right was my life's short-term goal.

So if some literary executor takes the time to pan for gold in the manuscripts and papers of a worthy poet, and makes a book out of the dust found there: fine. Should only a poem or two be truly good, that's a poem or two more than we had before. And it does remind us that every strong poem originally exists in the context of weaker poems: we poets do our best, but we're only human. If every third or fourth poem is a keeper, that's a decent-to-good major league batting average, and it's unrealistic to expect much better. It also reminds us that there's really no such thing as a *Complete* or *Collected Poems*: no gathering is truly exhaustive, and why should it be? Some effusions slip through the cracks, but that doesn't diminish the value of the poet's having written them in the first place, whether or not they ever resurface as "uncollected." They are the understory below the canopy poems, a necessary part of the ecosystem—patient, shade-tolerant, and often lovely in their own way.

MANUSCRIPT

One reason I still read the comics: They're a sanctuary for actual handwriting. Cartoonists lettered those words into those balloons or panels with their own inky hands.

I frequently have to explain to my students what "manuscript" means. They learned how to print their ABCs as children but never really had to practice or use cursive: from an early age, they were keyboarders, on computers and phones, and so having to write things down on paper must seem as archaic as taking up a quill to compose a billet-doux. Or as old-fashioned as a newspaper you hold in your hands and read. Or as antiquated as that peculiar arrangement of pages called a "book."

Is this a grievous loss, the disappearance of literal manuscript? Maybe not; most people's handwriting wasn't all that attractive. But it is another level of disconnection from the physical process of writing, which is felt more fully when pen moves over paper. It's another level of disembodiment, when the words we write exist as easily deletable 2-D flickers and not as made things in our 3-D world, ones that take more muscular effort to create or erase. It's another level of abstraction, when "manuscript" becomes merely metaphorical. And those levels of removal have emotional and maybe even moral or spiritual consequences.

I'm sure this is a minority opinion, one that—here in the high-speed twenty-first century—seems sentimental, retrograde, foolish. But having a hand is one of the glories of being human, and using it to write actual words on actual paper is the glory of glories. Manuscript means handwriting, and handwriting makes manuscript: for me, that slow, ancient process has always been a basic and necessary pleasure. There's a flow to it, but resistance is also involved, just enough friction to light the needed spark. It's as close as I get to holiness, there at my desk for a few hours: a good pen, some blank sheets, and my hand moving in the service of my imagination.

MARGINALIA

I was surprised—okay, dismayed—to find a stack of spiral-bound college notebooks at the back of a file cabinet drawer last week. How embarrassing, to look at my earnest notes taken with my earnest cartridge pen in my earnest A-student manner, back when I believed in the importance of being earnest...

I started ripping out pages, to recycle them, but then noticed something interesting about my English Literature of the 18th Century notes in the fall of 1976. Not the mimeographed handouts (still deliriously purple), not the saved exam books (how generous my teacher was), but the marginalia, the things I'd doodled when I should have been focusing on Pope or Swift, the sketches and drawings that brightened those neoclassical hours like daydreams. A Houyhnhnm saying, in its cartoon balloon, "And universal pickle buries all." Dr. Johnson, magnificently bewigged, his mouth hinting at a smile as he says, "Hi, I'm Ramblin' Sam."

Other notebooks from other courses taken over four-and-a-half years (two undergraduate, as a transfer-student English major, and two-and-a-half graduate, as a distracted M.A. in English Lit student) yielded other idle self-amusements. From a Shakespeare class: an ad for Stuckey's Pecan Divinity, with "There's a divinity that shapes our ends" on the wrapper. From a Renaissance class, taken during the lunch hour: a Hero and Leander sandwich, very like a sub. From an American Novel class: a view—from above—of a whale as a raft, titled, "Moby Finn." From a drama class: a meticulously-rendered cup of The Cherry Orchard yogurt. Plus drawings of blackboards, chairs, windows, and other classroom details, as well as the hair and clothes of those who sat in front of me: I seemed obsessed with one woman's bandana and the knot on the left strap of her sundress.

The longer I stayed in school, the less earnest the notetaking became, and the more elaborate the drawings grew. In a way, this was the last flourish of my graphic-art side: I'd started college at N.C. State's design school, and still loved to work with a pen, but my interests were shifting from the visual to the verbal as I took writing poetry more seriously. It was also surely a sign that I needed to stop pretending to be a very marginal scholar-in-training and get out of graduate school, which I soon did. But it was also evidence that the most interesting things sometimes happen at the margins, rather than at the (boring) center of whatever it is that Seems So Important at the Time. Those manual improvisations were looser, more associative and playful than the sober criticism I was reading and supposed to be writing. They were more like poetry, like the poems I was figuring out how to make.

On the back of the notebook of the last literature course I ever took, there's the usual assortment of quotes and sketches, and there's a huge cartoon balloon that clearly took a while to make. At its center is a drawing of a spindle choked with small papers jammed onto it, next to a toaster casting an enormous crosshatched shadow. The rest of the balloon is filled with this quote, rendered with calligraphic flair: "Each student who registers with the Career Placement Office will receive a FREE TOASTER to roast the host of rejection slips we can promise you'll receive as a MASTER OF ARTS!" I like how the words and drawing darkly conflate applying for jobs with submitting poems to magazines, which usually leads to some editor giving you the slip.

And right under that image of comic academic despair is this sentence, my future captured in tiny blue cursive, Flaubert speaking to me: "*Il faut écrire pour soi avant tout.*" That's what I really learned as a college student: *Above all, you must write for yourself.*

6.

BRIEFCASE

Some professors prefer bookbags, a more casual conveyance; some younger teachers use backpacks, like their students; some instructors fumble along with a slippery armload of bound or loose paper, without anything to stuff that stuff into.

I carry a briefcase, one made of black ballistic fabric, with several zippered pockets on the outside and more Velcroed compartments inside than a lightly organized poet requires. The pull-tabs and strap-clips jangle lightly as I walk down the hall. It's not a lawyer's stiff rectangular case, all leather and locks and hard edges, hauling evidence to court, files of guilt or innocence; it's solid but flexible, professional but not overly so, a teacherly carry-all for books, notes, pens, keys, tissues, spectacles, medication, anything that might be needed before returning to office or home.

When I walk into class and heave it up to the desk or table, it makes a satisfying thump, the first percussive note of a familiar overture. And—on a good day—when I open the flap and put my hand inside, I feel like a magician reaching into his magic hat, ready to pull out a new trick or two, to teach and to entertain the waiting audience.

GRADEBOOK

1.

I t's the topmost book I carry to every class.
Once my classroom desk is arranged—teaching notes, student work to be handed back, texts and books to be used that day—I pick up my gradebook and take roll. Early in the term, I must call every name, as I'm learning who's who; after a few weeks I can take attendance silently, by sight, before our meeting begins.

That gives me a written record of who was there, who was not, who was late, and how each student performed during the semester: poems, revisions, class participation, recitations, exams, reports, and extra credit. Not that my shorthand captures everything they did or said or were, but it provides enough that I can grade my students, or write them a letter of recommendation, or maybe remember them, ten, twenty, thirty-some years later, all because I took a few seconds to commit this daily data to paper, in ink, in this little book—this history—that they wrote with me.

2.

It's a Riggs' 18-Week College Record, bound in thick blue cardstock (a "four-ply Railroad Board cover"), with darker blue tape reinforcing its stapled spine, and with heavy white pages ruled in light blue lines for a day-to-day tallying of information. Once drop/add is over, and the class roster is finalized, I ink the students' names in my gradebook and tell them: "Okay. Now you're official."

The J. F. Riggs Publishing Company of Des Moines has been making "classroom records," as they call them, since 1893. In the twenty-first century, where electronic recordkeeping is the norm, these gradebooks are emphatically old-school.

As an archaic purveyor of educational material myself, I can't imagine teaching without one. I remember being handed my first Riggs' Class Record back in January 1977, when I was a second-semester graduate student at UNC preparing to teach my first course, a discussion section of Introduction to Film Criticism. I was thrilled to hold that gradebook in my hand: in some way, it meant I was a Real Teacher.

I don't know which Iowa genius decided on the 4.5 x 8-inch size, or the eighty-page format, but it's a perfect fit in the palm, in the pocket: it felt, and still feels, exactly right to me. It has heft, but not too much, like the kind of compact notebook a reporter or a writer might carry around. It's a book made for the hand, and filled by the hand.

3.

I still have that first gradebook—and every Riggs gradebook I've used since then, eight so far. (I took some instructional hiatuses in the 1980s; even so, it's a thick blue stack of records, more than 100 classes and 1,500 students.)

Do I still remember all those barely-younger-than-me people whose names I wrote so carefully, thirty-six springs ago, in the class roll on page two of book one? Do I still remember all the students I taught, and graded, in Greensboro and Ithaca and Appleton, before I landed back in Chapel Hill for good in 1990? Do I still remember all the Carolina undergraduates I've taught during the past several decades?

Certainly not. A lot of those names might as well be fictional, though they belong to actual flesh-and-blood people, real-life grown-up adults: all my students from the mid-1990s and earlier are older now than I was when I taught them. I'll never see or hear from most of them again. But it's satisfying, to their former teacher, to have this written-down version of their younger selves—first name, surname, a semester's work of marks following them like a long, fractured shadow composed of checks, tildes, x's, and a few letters from the beginning of the alphabet—in these books, these semi-permanent records, which also preserve versions of my younger self.

4.

My recordkeeping has gotten less spare and more detailed over the years. That may be a function of waning memory, and a need to save plenty of helpful details, but it's also a sign of my learning how to use the Riggs' College Record. Its perforated flaps—1.75-inch blank strips down the vertical outer margins of the pages—are a handy location for notes and footnotes and other jottings that fill out how a student is doing.

I've also made more use of the blank Teacher's Notes page at the back, especially for writing down some of the unintentionally delightful things my students say or write. A "bard owl." A poem "in turrets." (Tercets.) "Lent-filled pockets." "For all intensive purposes." "Type-rope walking." (Tightrope.) "The poem was chalk-full of imagery." "Knit-picky." "His whit was clearly visible." "The final buzzard sounds at the end of the game." As I tell them: Spell-check programs make poor proofreaders.

I've never been able to sustain a notebook or journal of my own—too much self-consciousness—but I think of these gradebooks as serving a similar role for the class itself: a place to compile daily facts and comments and observations that may later prove useful. Or entertaining. Or both.

5.

A few years back, one of my younger colleagues—a fellow lover of the traditional blue gradebooks, who'd seen me using one when teaching her senior Honors poetry class—heard a rumor that Riggs was going to stop making them. She was so distressed that she ordered enough to see her through the rest of her teaching career. This was a not-inconsiderable investment, since she was still in her twenties.

She kindly let me buy enough of the 18-Week College Records to take me to retirement, now in the near distance. They're waiting on a shelf in my office, stiff and unbroken-in, unlike my finger-smudged, corner-bent, inked-full and retired gradebooks, veterans of educational scrimmage through many academic years.

It's peculiar, to look at those few unused blue books and to think that, once they're filled, I won't be walking into any more classrooms on the first day, reading the temporary roll ("Tell me if you want to be called something other than what the university calls you"), and beginning another semester's sojourn with a group of aspiring writers whose names will soon end up in my gradebook, who will always have at least one thing in common: our class.

I don't know what will happen to these records, these manuscripts, these memorials of our meetings and the work that came out of them. It's not like schools keep an archive of gradebooks—who besides the teacher might care about such things, really? Where have all those names and marks and numbers gone, through the recording generations? I don't want to think about the answers to those questions.

6.

Some of my former students have become my friends. Some have gotten married, and I've attended their weddings, even reading a poem as part of several ceremonies. Some have had children, and I may soon start to teach those kids, as—years ago—I began to teach the children of my college friends, a peculiar sensation at first, but increasingly gratifying.

Some of my former students have had a hard time of it: depression, addiction, poverty. Some have died: climbing accident, car crash, other untimely fates. I've written the parents whose children passed far too young, and I've told them what a pleasure it was to have their daughter or son in my classes, a truth I know in my heart but something I can also behold in my gradebooks, which tell me— to the day—how well he did on this, how hard she worked on that, how we spent our time together. I'm not sure anything can help with such unimaginable loss, but I hope this does, a bit.

7.

Looking back through these gradebooks, I'm surprised by how clearly I recall some of the classes, a particularly fortunate (or, rarely, unfortunate) combination of personalities and ability and spirit. And I can remember a student or two from my earliest days on the other side of the desk: one, a devoted hacky-sack player in the quad outside the English building, began the semester by declaring Jim Morrison the greatest poet of the twentieth century, then trashed his classmates' poems during the first workshop. When it was finally time for us to discuss one of his poems, naturally everyone found plenty to cut and fix, with surgical precision, including a shy girl who hadn't spoken in class so far: at that point, he violated the authorial Gag Rule, stood up, pointed at her, and cried: "And you— you—you probably *eat the flesh of animals!*" He stomped out, never came to class again, and (thanks to his seventeen absences, in fall 1984) earned a memorable F.

Sometimes one of my former students will get in touch out of nowhere. A member of my fall 1978 film criticism class—now a successful lawyer in Charlotte—wrote a few years ago to see if his son, a prospective student, could visit a Creative Writing class. "I still mark margins with those lines and checkmarks you used," he said, about his annotating of cases and briefs. You never know what a student will remember, what practice or habit of yours might be carried on.

On the happy day when I hear from a McFee alum, I'm reminded that each class is a community, and that those communities continue through time. My gradebooks are censuses of those groups, brought together by an interest in poetry and a desire to write it, and their rolls will never be expunged. I don't sit down and read my Riggs' 18-week college records for pleasure—not yet, anyway—but every time I open one, I come across a name that makes me smile, with pleasure for the person, for what was imagined and written and revised and then recorded in this little blue book, and for the brief time we shared in the service of the word, not so long ago.

HANDOUTS

Each semester begins with a handout: the syllabus, the table of contents for the term, each class a passage in the book that teacher and students compose together. And it proceeds by handouts as well, ones I've photocopied on a departmental machine, front and back if possible, then paper-clipped together and brought to class to pass around, each student taking one copy then passing the diminishing stack to the left till the last one is taken by the student to my immediate right. Circle closed. Here we go.

"Workshops are an exercise in paper management," I tell my poets, advising them to get a capacious envelope or notebook for transporting and storing the sheets they will collect, all those servings of literary dishes passed around our metaphorical table. In a recent Introduction to Poetry Writing class, I gave them handouts on exemplary poems, memorization and recitation, titles, thinking metaphorically, figurative language, scansion, places of sound articulation in the mouth, couplets, tercets, revision, other voices, contemporary English sonnets, villanelles, pantoums, and sestinas, as well as the syllabus, a list of reserve reading books, a map of "places to find poetry in Chapel Hill," the midterm, and the term poem requirements. I hoped that each of those pieces of paper might bring them some measure of information, instruction, and inspiration.

I require my students to print out copies of each poem they write, so that their classmates can have it in hand to read, and re-read, and mark up as helpfully and specifically as possible. ("This is the golden rule of workshop," I say: "Critique as you would be critiqued.") Together, the handouts and the poems—their own and others'—compose the class's real textbook, and it's a substantial one.

Could this all be done electronically? I suppose so. Is it just a waste of paper and ink and trees, then? I hope not. I think it's important to put your hand out and take the poem, to receive and accept it, to touch and hold it, to close the gap between yourself and that body of written words with your own actual physical body—fingertips, fingers, palm, wrist, arm, shoulder, neck, head, eyes, ears, brain. I think it helps to have a sheet of poetry that you can consult any time of the day or night, simply by lifting your eyelids and reading. Can those handouts be ignored or forgotten? Sure. Can they be thrown away or lost? Undoubtedly. But they do literally exist: they are a sensory fact in our three-dimensional world, if only for a little while. And to a young writer who really needs them, sometimes they may matter as much as a donation of food or clothing or money.

Last week, I was talking with several friends who had been students of mine in an Intermediate Poetry Writing workshop in 1994. I was delighted to hear that they still had the handouts I'd so carefully assembled and copied for their classes, those poetic selections I thought would enlighten and delight them, the course's homemade anthology. In the decades since, those handouts have changed—I keep updating and, I hope, improving them—and I currently have more than a hundred files that I can e-mail as Microsoft Word documents, which wasn't an option in the mid-1990s. I still prefer the paper versions, though, and I actually have some of the handouts from my own undergraduate classes: the oldest ones, mimeographs, have faded to near-invisibility, and their damp, illicit smell evaporated long ago, but I can make out the faint purple words I thought worth saving, if I squint at them in the right light. I don't remember what those late professors said, day by day by day, but it's a pleasure to hold their old handouts in my hands.

WORKSHOP

I once had a fussy literature colleague who winced at not only the term "creative writing" but also at the word "workshop," particularly its verb forms, "to workshop" or "workshopping."

Me, I've always liked that durable compound—the nuts-and-boltsiness of it, the hands-on quality it embodies, the fact that it begins with "work" and so reminds my sometimes dreamy student-poets what writing is, above all. One learns to handle things carefully in a workshop, whether a bandsaw or a simile, and the more the worker practices, the more skilled he becomes as a maker.

Each workshop is different, depending on the poems and poets under discussion, but all of mine begin the same way: with the writers passing around paper copies of their new work. Once each student has all the poems in hand, and before we begin to inspect and appreciate and possibly repair them, we go around the room and hear the author read aloud—without comment or explanation—what he or she wrote and rewrote and copied and brought to class, while we look at it on the page.

To me, that's when the workshop really begins: in words coming from mouths, in writers and listeners feeling those phonemes inhabit their bodies. The ear will tell you things that the eye and brain, those darlings of the classroom, simply can't. In the air, you will catch verbal weaknesses that you hadn't imagined, and you may also discover loveliness you hadn't known was there. I ask each student to read the poem slowly, carefully, honoring the words and phrases and lines and breaks and stanzas as they appear on the page; and I ask the next student in the read-around to let the previous poem resonate in silence for a few seconds, like a well-struck chord, before continuing.

It's often my favorite part of workshop, those group readings. The room is hushed and attentive, as the players tune their concert A's. It's a tender time, before the tools come out. But the tools must come out, as we work together to make the work even better.

Before workshopping proper starts, I ask another class member to read the poem chosen for discussion: it helps to hear your poem in somebody else's voice. Once we've said what needs to be said, the students pass their written comments back to the author. I know that those comments vary widely in their accuracy and helpfulness; I know that each poet whose poem has been workshopped gets contradictory advice; I know that some workshop members don't write their comments down until they get to class, if then. But I also know—from my own experience, as a student and later as the teacher—that some extremely insightful things can get said and noted by your classmates, things that really do show you how to revisit what you've written and then improve it.

That requires more work, of course. Etymologically, "working" means "doing," as "poetry" means "making," and I like the practical, unpretentious roots of those words. Some wayward things may be said during workshops, but—with the author silent, listening to the comments; with the class members addressing specific details and issues in the poem, not uttering vague generalities; and with me trying to guide the discussion as efficiently as I can— the words we say and write about our fellow poets' words often lead to stronger writing, in revisions and also in future poems whose making may have been influenced by our workshop.

HOMEWORK

The companion word to "workshop," though with "work" at the other end, "homework" provides a private balance to that more public noun.

Creative writing classes may not have homework assignments in the traditional sense, e.g., pages to read and master and be tested on; but in a way, such classes are nothing but homework, in that what you do at home determines everything, not merely the course grade, or the quality of poems brought into workshop, but your very fate as a writer. If you don't learn to work hard on your own—practicing the three phonetic *r*'s I preach to my students: *reading* others' poems, *writing* your own poetry, then *revising* it—then you're probably not going to become or stay a poet.

Some homework can seem like mere busy work, inessential tasks that the teacher inflicts on you. A writer's homework, self-assigned, is the exact opposite. Learning how to do it, and to keep doing it, is a lifelong course of study, pursued but never mastered. Sometimes that labor, invisible to others, may seem tedious; sometimes the drafts and rewrites may be pure unselfconscious joy; but you have to put in the time at home to bring your best work—your most fully realized literary self—into the world.

OFFICE HOURS

Twice a week, I'm in my campus office with the door open for an hour and a quarter, ready to do one thing only: receive guests. Now and then a student comes by to discuss recent or future work, or a colleague drops in to chat for a few minutes; but often it's just me in my office, for the announced official hours but also for the hours before and after class when I come back to that base to re-group, to check messages, and to have a little private time when I'm not talking to others.

I do schedule student conferences during the semester, around mid-term at least. That's the only time I see many of them outside the classroom, and it's interesting to find out how they will behave, one on one. I'm a little more relaxed and forthcoming in the privacy of 416 Greenlaw, and usually they are, too. It's like having them visit a version of my home, where books crowd the shelves ("Have you actually *read* all those?"), and art—mostly framed poetry broad-sides—brightens the walls, and bric-a-brac decorates most every surface: a baseball found under the bleachers in Cooperstown, the pâpier-maché head of a former chancellor that my son made and wore one Halloween, and (stuck to file cabinets, walls, and printers) postcards that former students have sent me from around the world. It's a comfortable place, by design, for my sake but also for theirs: they can sit in the rocking chair, and take a break, and talk about their work or whatever is on their mind or in their heart. Sometimes there are tears. I keep a box of tissues close to hand.

I remember being fascinated by the concept of office hours when I was an undergraduate, by the thought that a rube like me could meet with an eminent scholar or writer simply by showing up between the hours of x and y, "or by appointment." What a gift! Sure, some of the profs were less hospitable than others—one isolate kept his hours from 7 to 8 A.M. MWF, and another's office was so ominously devoid of books or any human touch that you didn't really want to be in there—but most of my teachers were kind and attentive, and made me feel that I was part of the intellectual society of the university.

Office hours felt, and feel, like a middle ground between the compressed minutes of a classroom and the expansive flow of time beyond campus. They are, like writing hours themselves, a time apart—private, intense yet relaxed, serious fun. I always keep them posted on a card taped to my door, so that anyone who wants to see me knows exactly when I'll be there, and can take a seat on the bench across from 416, ready for our conversation to begin.

THE BLACKBOARD

1.

I start the first class of each semester by walking into the room, picking up a piece of chalk from the tray, and writing my name, then the course name, on the blackboard. Which means that I begin each term by facing the blackboard, not the class.

Which is just how I like it. I lift my right arm, as if in greeting, as if to say, *Here we are again, old friend. Here's the latest word in our long, dusty story.*

And I—we—begin to write.

2.

The blackboard is part of a classroom's theater, part of the stage for a teacher's performance.

One of my improvisatory colleagues begins his classes by trying to use any writing left behind on the blackboard by the previous teacher, whatever the topic.

Another ends the hour by tossing the piece of chalk over his shoulder, flat against the blackboard, where it falls straight down into the tray as he exits the classroom.

I wish I could be so showy. Though I often write something on the board in lower-level classes, the only drama involved is my erasing it once the period is done, leaving ghosts of my hand to haunt the next performance of teacher and students in that space, the latest lines in a palimpsest of professorial scrawls.

3.

My stylish third-grade teacher had an adjustable metal holder into which she inserted the cartridge of chalk, so she wouldn't get as much dust on her fingertips and painted nails.

My elementary-school music teacher had a device—with an oak handle and parallel clasping wires—that held five sticks of chalk, allowing her to draw a musical staff with one long, smooth backhand swipe, lines to which she then affixed time signatures, notes, and bars.

At my twenty-first century university, which keeps pouring money into pricey, computerized "master classrooms," sometimes there's no chalk in the tray, and I must go search for it, across or down the hall. But I don't mind having to dig up a stick or a stub, and I appreciate what it leaves on my fingers: it's like having saw-dust on your skin after working with wood, a sign of honest indus-try.

4.

If we were indolent, or sassy, or otherwise badly behaved in the grade-school classroom, our teachers might send us outside after school, to "beat out" the erasers.

I know this was supposed to be punitive, a stern dust-to-dust lesson, but I always enjoyed creating little yellow clouds by smack-ing those tight felt pads against the side of the school, or by clap-ping two erasers together in front of me and watching the residue of Mrs. Sizemore's lessons float away on the breeze.

5.

The stick of fresh chalk like a thick cigarette between my fin-gers.

The arid, informational smell of the dust it made.

The one tall wall I was ever allowed to write on.

The scratch of chalk against blackboard making the stick slightly shorter, angling the tip so I had to rotate the cylinder as I wrote, to keep its point sharp.

The screech of chalk wielded poorly against board, or of fingernails slowly drawn across it, and the gratifying winces or squeals behind me.

6.

Blackboards are a substantial fact in the classroom, their huge fixed-to-the-wall panels looming over us, daring somebody to come touch them. Writing on blackboards in real time leaves an actual mark. And the word *blackboard* itself is a solid bilabial outburst, like *blackbird* or *backboard*.

But what we write on blackboards is ephemeral. And they're ignored unless used, their dark blankness like unlit windows at night.

7.

Some teachers raised writing on the blackboard to a high level of craft, if not art.

Mrs. Ponder, Mrs. Sparks, Mrs. Franklin, Mrs. Hoke, Mrs. Allen, Mrs. Moore, all those older married ladies at Valley Springs School in Skyland, North Carolina: they never seemed to tire of executing perfect Palmer Method cursive, hoping their example would inspire us mountain children to improve our rustic handwriting.

Professor John Reuer at N.C. State's School of Design: in his History of Architecture class, Dr. Reuer lettered information on the lecture-hall board with the precision of a draftsman perfecting a blueprint, in stylized capitals that he frequently erased and rewrote (muttering in German) because the angle or spacing wasn't precisely right. I'll never forget the Bauhaus beauty of his M's and W's.

And Father Devereux, in Renaissance English Literature at UNC: he'd whistle his way into class and then start writing on the board in an elegant italic hand, a challenging task performed with effortless *sprezzatura*—a word I learned from him, one that I will always associate with that cheerful Jesuit.

I try to slow down, to emulate those patient scribes, whose writing on blackboards now seems as archaic as cave art executed in charcoal by torchlight. I try to honor their measured hand in my fitful slanting one. Though I fail, I hope there's a faint echo of those late teachers' chalkwork in mine.

8.

Every teacher's epitaph could be a version of Keats's:
Here lies one whose name was writ on blackboards.

9.

Once upon a time, the threat to blackboards was greenboards, or whiteboards, or whatever new product was currently being peddled to schools as a way of avoiding dusty chalk and erasers, as well as boards you had to wash. But those modern technologies introduced their own problems—for example, the price of a special erasable-ink marker as opposed to a cheap stick of processed gypsum (i.e., blackboard chalk). And if someone mistakenly used a permanent pen on the dry-erase surface: uh-oh.

These days, old-school blackboards are being supplanted by computerized "learning management systems" like Blackboard Inc., whose software makes it possible to get information to classes without teachers ever lifting chalk to board. That may be ideal for big lecture courses, where speed and quantity of transmission are primary, and students have their laptops—the postmodern pupils' writing slates, their personal e-chalkboards—open to receive such data. And some of my creative writing colleagues are using Blackboard or Sakai or Dropbox to share material with our much smaller classes, or for the students to post and respond to one another's work.

I may end up doing that, but for the time being I'm sticking with the non-electronic blackboard. Why? Partly because we've been together for thirty-five years, and familiarity has not yet bred contempt. Partly because I like the tactile, uncomplicated, almost primitive way it works. But mostly I want to keep using the blackboard because it keeps each class's community physically in the classroom and not online. It's the communal slate on which we write, and it's a good thing for teacher and students to see each other actually doing that. It's humanly important to write words with our hands and arms and whole bodies, for a few minutes twice a week at least, and not just type them with busy digits and thumbs, all day every day.

10.

Many people have bad feelings about blackboards. When Rosa Lee Baldwin stared down one of us high-school smart-alecks and summoned us to the board to solve a tricky geometry problem, our hearts sank like a negative slope. Bart Simpson's writing on the blackboard at the beginning of each episode of *The Simpsons*—funny as it is: "Cursive writing does not mean what I think it does" or "I am not delightfully saucy"—is in fact punishment, one from which he's freed by the ringing bell. And I know one professor who avoids blackboards completely, lest he inadvertently rub up against the chalk tray and leave a dusty line across the back of his pants.

When I turn 180 degrees and face the blackboard, I'm not thinking about my butt or Bart or adolescent traumas. If I'm thinking at all, it may be something like, *Just look at all this empty space!* That prospect might fill me with dread, in a gray mood, but most days I find something comforting in lifting my hand and brightening those big black pages with clusters of words.

11.

Writing on a blackboard is, above all, writing. It is committing manuscript, on a flat surface, though what you're writing on is a vertical, reusable wall panel and not a sheet of paper horizontal on a desk. Writing on a blackboard is like writing a letter or a poem by hand: for one class period, what you've written—those yellow or white lines, those words or numbers or marks, that chalked text—is your holograph.

Then it goes away. Like all writing. Like us.

Except it doesn't, not totally. Because other people have read it, as the words emerged from your hand like a magic trick, and may remember it. Because a few of your students may have written down some of what you wrote down, their copies echoing your original. Because writing begets writing.

12.

I begin some classes by walking in, putting down my briefcase, and writing a quote on the blackboard, some pithy utterance from a fellow writer appropriate to what we're working on that day. I've collected thousands of such sayings through the decades, and it's fun to share them with my students.

I could simply read those quotes aloud to the class—that would be quicker, obviously—but I don't think it would be as memorable. Taking the time to form letters and words, one by one, in front of the class, while students watch the phrase or sentence unfold, followed by the author's name, seems worth my effort. That way, the quote doesn't merely disappear into academic air: it lingers on the blackboard for seventy-five minutes, hanging over my head as we talk, an epigraph for this new chapter of our semester's work-

in-progress, something for a student to consider, or absorb indirect-
ly as we give our attention to other words, or notice as I'm erasing it
with a gesture that's almost tender, a farewell wave.

7.

SLOW DOWN

One thing I've always loved about poetry: it makes you slow down.

You can't—or, more accurately, shouldn't—rush the writing of a poem. It needs to take its time, gather momentum and necessity, work its way toward words. If you force it onto the page too quickly, you may end up with something that's interesting in part or to a degree, but it won't be what it could have been, a fully-ripened poem, which can take months, or years, or decades to mature. A poet can tell when that happens, when verbal patience has paid off and the result is It, the truly real thing, a poem that exists not because you worried it into being but because it came through you when it had to, when it was ready, when you were willing to slow down and wait for it.

You can't—or, more accurately, shouldn't—rush the reading of a poem either. Poetry is the opposite of speed reading: it's slow-motion reading, where you're allowed to take your time and savor the text in depth, its sounds, its movement, its concentrated and implicit nature. There's no need to hurry through, searching for information that can be used, like answers to a quiz: poetry doesn't (or shouldn't be asked to) work that way. The pleasures afforded by reading poetry are qualitative, not quantitative. That's one reason I always encourage my students to read a poem aloud, to let it work in the oral cavity and the inner ear, in the lungs and the gut, as well as in the overvalued gray matter.

Which means that writing and reading poems is a subversive activity, in this time when instantaneous access and exchange are everything. Such speediness certainly has its uses, but I'm not sure they have much to do with poetry. Where's the fire? You should write or read a poem in the same way that you'd eat a good meal, or have a nice drink, or perform any other significantly pleasurable human activity: not like you're wolfing down fast food, or gulping down Gatorade, but with your senses and intellect as attentive as possible to what is happening. You should be focused but also relaxed, alert but leisurely, serious but playful. And such a paradoxical state requires, first of all, that you simply slow down.

EMPLOYMENT

We writers are never unemployed. There may be times when we don't have a "job," making a "living wage," but we are always employed—every waking minute of every day, and some sleeping minutes—as writers, creatures who cannot help watching, listening, thinking, then converting the world to words and/or inventing a world in words.

Once we discover and accept that we must write, writing becomes our full-time job, our actual living wage. That becomes our real work, which must be undertaken with as much of our being as we can muster; otherwise, we are not fully inhabiting the life we want and need and are meant to live.

We writers must put actual food on the table and pay real rent, like everybody else. Like everybody else, we find ways to get paid so that we can. But those positions and paychecks are merely means to an end. The end, the goal, the point of it all is always one thing: Writing. That is our true employment.

GUILTY

How do you deal with the guilt of being a writer, when you're a lapsed Southern Baptist from the working class, and when your wife leaves for the office every weekday before 8 A.M.?

Believe me, I know: writing is work, it's hard work, it's difficult and demanding work, in a way that most jobs aren't. It requires regular effort over many years to produce something that others (a few others) may (just may) want to read. Punching the literary time clock is no guarantee of success, much less income: in a way, is there any harder work than what writers and other artists do?

Maybe not. But still: I'm here at home and my wife is across town, working all-out, all day. I can get up from my desk and go brew a cup of tea, but she can't. I can stretch languidly and stare out the window and stroll to the mailbox, but she can't. What I do doesn't look much like work, and it sure doesn't feel like spot-welding or house-painting or cataloguing library books, a few of the menial things I've done for money in the past.

Many years ago, a neighborhood lady—noticing that my car was often in the driveway when other men were off at their jobs—asked this of my mother-in-law, with whom she went to church: "Now, Michael does not work at all, is that correct?" She wasn't being catty, she was simply looking to confirm what she had observed. And though my mother-in-law must have reported this story to me, I don't know what her answer was. "Yes, that is correct"?

I do teach, and that does take me and my car away from the house, even if my schedule isn't as regular as a daily 9-to-5 routine. But that doesn't assuage my guilt very much. Teaching well, like writing well, is deceptively hard; believe me, I know. But honestly: which is more onerous, leading a creative writing workshop and annotating undergraduate poems, or seeing an overload of patients or negotiating with difficult clients or working another shift at a crummy minimum-wage job?

When carpenters and painters are in the house, I feel guilty about sitting at my computer typing while they saw and hammer and prime and sweat. I feel guilty when my wife comes home from the office, exhausted: I may try to look busy, or impress her with the minor housework I've spent a few minutes on, but that's a ruse. I don't question the value of what I do, or whether I should be doing it: no doubt, I've found my vocation and I'm striving to fulfill it. It's not like writing is a crime: I'm not doing anything wrong, committing poems. But sometimes—when I step back from it, and look at what I do in the context of what other working Americans do—I must admit: I feel guilty.

VOICE

A friend recently heard Paul Simon sing, and said she enjoyed it but preferred "his younger voice." He probably does, too, but at age seventy-one there's not much to be done about it: older vocal cords become weaker and drier, and what comes out of the chest and throat and mouth sounds thinner, narrower in range, increasingly strained—a sad fate for a singer, but one that all humans share.

"Voice" is an ambiguous literary quality. Young poets are often obsessed with "finding their voice," a sound uniquely and authentically theirs, so that readers will recognize it as different from all other voices. But who knows how such a thing happens, exactly, and when? It's hardly a conscious process or decision—you write, and rewrite, and keep singing new songs, for years and years and years, until what comes out seems truly you.

And then you keep on singing, in this voice you've made or discovered or inherited, and you keep challenging yourself to try new things with it, changing while remaining faithful to this particular sound that is you. No poet should want to make a career of delivering the same song in the same manner. Meanwhile, time is having its way with the body through which your words flow: what once came with relative ease frequently requires more effort, and feels like a muffled version of your youthful self.

So what? Why keep trying to sound like a twenty-five-year-old? Your voice is still in you—which is to say, your voice is still you—as long as you have breath: make adjustments, work with what you have, and never stop singing.

Like Paul Simon with his records, your voicings have a certain permanence, even if they're not exactly immortal. That written embodiment of yourself will exist once you don't, and interested readers can continue to hear and admire its peculiar combination of vowels and consonants, of phrasing and line and stanza, of rhythm and timing and momentum, all those instinctive oral/aural maneuvers that made up your voice, which was—and is, and ever shall be—as distinctive and mysterious as your DNA, or your fingerprints, or the handwriting that you kept practicing until one day it was finally you.

AUDIENCE

I have a single reader that I'm sure of, and—believe me—he's a nitpicker, impossible to please.

IMMORTALITY

Writers wield such flimsy materials for immortality—the ink that fades, the paper that yellows or crumbles or burns, the books that waste away on dusty shelves, unread. And the electronic versions of our word-selves are likewise subject to decay, becoming unrecognizable by subsequent technologies or disappearing as dead links.

Not to mention the human unlikeliness of any work living forever—the heart that shifts to other loves, the mind whose grasp on language slackens, the fickleness of reputation during one's lifetime, much less afterwards. "Out of sight, out of mind" almost always trumps "Absence makes the heart grow fonder."

Why should writers want to be immortal, anyway, any more than you'd want to live forever in a mortal body? Maybe it's best to write as well as you can for a while, to enjoy the satisfactions that writing may bring, and then to step aside and let another writer take your place. Maybe it's better not to linger in anthologies after you're gone, an example of a now-unfashionable style, once-common words and references weighted down by explicatory footnotes. Maybe it's a good thing, embracing your expiration date, like expecting to be rejected when submitting to a magazine: then if you get an acceptance, and people read you in print—terrific, what a bonus!

Well, perhaps. But it's also true that writers—creatures who have always been hyperconscious of their mortality—hope that their poems and stories and novels will take on a life outside them, beyond them, without them. I don't mean something as grand as "Poetry redeems from decay the visitations of the divinity in man," that degree of everlastingness. I just mean this: the possibility of one's work continuing to be read and reread by people in the future,

MICHAEL McFEE   221

against all literary odds. Though a writer doesn't count on it and can't predict it, such immortality would be a surprise and a delight, a heaven to strive for, even if it may not exist.